THE SEALED TRUTH

Dr. William R. Holland

iUniverse, Inc.
Bloomington

The Sealed Truth

Copyright © 2011 Dr. William R. Holland

All rights reserved. No part of this book may be used or reproduced by any means, graphic, electronic, or mechanical, including photocopying, recording, taping or by any information storage retrieval system without the written permission of the publisher except in the case of brief quotations embodied in critical articles and reviews.

iUniverse books may be ordered through booksellers or by contacting:

iUniverse
1663 Liberty Drive
Bloomington, IN 47403
www.iuniverse.com
1-800-Authors (1-800-288-4677)

Because of the dynamic nature of the Internet, any Web addresses or links contained in this book may have changed since publication and may no longer be valid. The views expressed in this work are solely those of the author and do not necessarily reflect the views of the publisher, and the publisher hereby disclaims any responsibility for them.

Any people depicted in stock imagery provided by Thinkstock are models, and such images are being used for illustrative purposes only.

Certain stock imagery © Thinkstock.

ISBN: 978-1-4620-1252-7 (pbk)
ISBN: 978-1-4620-1253-4 (ebk)

Printed in the United States of America

iUniverse rev. date: 4/14/2011

This book is dedicated to Jane Doherty and other parents who have suffered the grief and agony of having a missing child. There is no greater pain.

Author's Note

The Sealed Truth is a based on a gruesome crime of the kidnapping and murder of a five year old, freckled-faced, blond-haired boy in a small village in southern Rhode Island in 1975.

The storyline flows from the true crime, but names and locations mentioned in the book have been changed to protect the identity and preserve the privacy of all characters.

Conjecture and poetic license were used in certain areas since certain facts were unknown and different interpretations of what actually happened exit. The book is therefore not meant to be a totally accurate rendition of this heinous crime that continues to haunt local residents to this very day.

Only two or three minor characters, scenes and dialogue were products of the author's imagination. The book is therefore mainly non-fiction based on a true crime story.

The major part of the book's content was gathered directly from actual police files and records of the case and personal interviews with over sixty people. Although the names are changed and the setting is a fictitious small town in Massachusetts, the police interviews and information provided by other individuals were a result of actual taped interviews or conversations with real people in the Rhode Island community where the crime occurred. Quotations from newspaper articles were also taken from the local Rhode Island newspapers and are acknowledged at the end of the book.

In writing the book I sought answers to following questions: Why did a lonely young man turn into a child killer? What might have triggered his "going over the edge" and becoming a violent psychopath? Why were police and others so blind to the possibility of his being a suspect? Is there any truth to the persistent rumors about the alleged gruesome and unspeakable things the killer did to the kidnapped boy after he killed him? And finally, how did the victims cope with such tragedy?

Books of this nature very seldom report the exact truth, and speculation is unavoidable. The passage of time and the need to respect the sensibilities of the actual victims makes it difficult to unveil the full truth. In many cases, new questions emerge, questions that need further investigation and may never be answered.

However, the book does answer one question. Because the book covers a period of thirty-six years, there was an opportunity to determine the residual effect this horrific crime had on the victims, not only at the time of the crime, but also many years later.

I have been asked why I would write such a disturbing book. My answer is simple. Our children are more at risk today than they were in the 1970's. With the advent of the Internet and the continuance of weak and ineffective sexual predator laws, the number of young children being exploited by sexual molesters is on the rise. As someone who has been directly involved in the firing of school personnel for sexual assault of school children, and has dealt with sexual abuse and the stalking of school children by sexual predators in the community, I can attest to the fact that our children are more vulnerable to sexual exploitation today than they have ever been.

This book intends to serve one major purpose. It tells parents that taking all means humanly possible to protect their children from harm is not silly overprotection that damages a child's psyche. If we are to keep our children out of harm's way, the loving concern and constant vigilance by parents are absolute imperatives in today's society.

Unfortunately, because of the confluence of circumstances that cannot be predicted or controlled, tragedies like the one described in this book will occur again. Yet with our increased awareness such crimes will be fewer, and a greater number of potential crimes will be averted, before violence strikes and results in the heartbreaking loss of human life.

One lady quoted in the book put it best, "Many people walk around with strange exteriors and twisted, broken interiors—few strike out at society and commit violence the way Justin Doherty's killer did. Unfortunately, the killer lived among us and we didn't recognize him."

Agreed, the book will not be an easy one to read. As one senior editor who read the manuscript said, "This is not the type of book to be enjoyed. It's a disturbing story of a terrible crime. It's provocative, makes the reader think, and will probably make them be determined to be a little more careful and a little more protective of their children."

PART ONE

Chapter 1

Sunday, May 18, 1975, was an outright gorgeous day—crystal blue sky, unseasonably warm, the type of day that youngsters' relish and mothers welcome, particularly after a cold, rainy spring.

A little after noontime, five-year-old Justin Doherty, his six-year-old brother Joey, and seven-year-old sister Robin were ushered out the door by their mother Jane to play with their Suffork Street friends as she cleaned the house and prepared for an early family dinner to celebrate her twenty-fifth birthday.

Suffork Street was a working class neighborhood of young families in Hopeville, a town in western Massachusetts, outside of Springfield. Cape Cod style houses lined both sides of the street on lots so narrow that it was impossible to build more than a one-car garage on their property. The majority of houses were mill homes built in the late nineteenth century and early twentieth century by George Suffork, a local landowner and contractor, whose great granddaughter and her family still lived in the old white colonial family homestead at the bottom of the street.

Even though the houses were crammed together on narrow lots and resembled row houses, they were located close enough to the street to provide for decent sized backyards where clusters of active young children played and families often gathered for neighborhood barbecues.

One saving grace for the thirty or so youngsters who lived on the street was an empty lot right next to the Doherty house, which they nicknamed "Tracey Field," since it was on young Charlie Tracey's property. Except for a few teenagers, most of the kids were quite young, separated by three or four years at the most. As one neighbor put it, "In those years we had a lot of little ones running in and out of our yards all the time."

Tracey Field was like an overactive magnet, where youngsters were quickly drawn to play football, baseball, and other spirited games on a daily basis, in good weather or in bad, when young bodies sought the special sensation of flying recklessly into inviting puddles and later returning to their homes looking like warriors returning from a muddy battlefield. Suffork Street was a great place for children to grow up with plenty of playmates, family parties, and friendly neighbors—a place where everyone knew and looked out for one another.

Justin and Joey anxiously ran out the back door and headed for Tracy Field to find their buddies while Robin remained in her backyard playing with two girlfriends who had just walked up to her house. The two Doherty boys played with other children in the field for a while, but grew restless because, surprisingly, none of their closest buddies were there that day. One neighborhood mother remembered a bored Justin crossing the street wanting to play with her four-year old daughter. Unfortunately, the mother had other plans for her and brought her inside. She gently told Justin, "Go on home."

Looking for some fun, Joey and Justin decided to walk down Suffork to Center Street, past the red brick Hopeville fire station and over to the recently constructed low income housing project, where they met three slightly older friends. As Jane Doherty would later recall, "Both of my boys were allowed to walk to the fire station, which was a few feet from the bottom of Suffork because their father was a volunteer there."

During the course of the afternoon, a rock-throwing incident involving boys in the project occurred. Joey decided to return home afterward, but Justin remained. Jane later explained, "When Joey came home he was whining about the other kids throwing rocks, so I told him to go back and get his brother. Well, Joey wouldn't go get him because he was afraid he would get hit by stones."

According to the police reports of two detectives who later interviewed Joey, three children from the project, and one parent who had observed the boys playing, Justin left the project shortly after his brother at approximately 5 p.m. The parent and the playmates recall seeing a contented Justin walking down the driveway toward Center Street and, about halfway down, slipping through a hole in the wire fence behind the fire station. They said the last time they saw him he was walking past the telephone booth in front of the Wayside Bar and heading for the lower part of Suffork Street.

In the coming weeks, police interviewed numerous individuals who lived in the project, worked in the bar, or happened to be in the area of the bar and fire station at approximately the same time Justin began his walk home. A buxom, red-haired ice cream lady known for the colorful tattoos that covered her sizeable arms was questioned because her truck was seen in the area of the bar sometime Sunday afternoon. Neighbors and bar patrons and owners of businesses nearby were also interviewed. The following Sunday, police even set up roadblocks on Center Street, stopping cars in the hope that some drivers might have seen Justin the previous Sunday. But no one else had seen Justin Doherty as he headed for home that afternoon—and no one would ever see him again.

Chapter 2

He pushed the broken shade aside and peered out the front window of his dark house, he spotted young Justin Doherty walking up Suffork Street. Except for Justin, the street looked deserted. His neighbors were nowhere to be seen, the cars that usually clogged their driveways were gone. No children were playing in Tracey Field or even in nearby backyards. Where was everyone on this balmy, Sunday afternoon?

Visiting friends, picnicking at the lake, eating at the Hopeville Diner or Sally's Restaurant? Who knows or cares?

He knew one thing. He was finally alone in his house and would be for some time. The three adults who lived in the small house with him were visiting relatives and would not be back until later that night. It was a perfect opportunity to act out one of his bizarre fantasies; something most aspiring actors would never would experience—the thrill of actually killing someone, learning what it feels like, and having complete dominance over someone else. His cravings bubbled out of control as he watched Justin about to pass the front of his house.

He had recently wondered what it would be like to commit the perfect crime. He'd read many gory crime novels and participated in several plays where he played the role of a murderer. He enjoyed reading Greek mythology and was fascinated with stories about characters who committed all types of atrocities. He planned on acting one day in his own mystery play. He thought he could gain incredible new insight into how a killer feels when he murders someone. It would be fun.

He knew he could easily outwit the police. He was too smart to be caught since they all were incompetent. He had given considerable thought to exactly how he would kill a neighborhood boy, any young boy he could overpower physically and sexually and easily dispose of the remains.

As Justin approached his house, he quietly said "Hey, Justin, over here."

Justin was a shy child, and although he knew and recognized his caller, he usually ignored him, as did most of the other kids in his neighborhood. This time, however, Justin unfortunately didn't ignore him.

"Would you like to see a real policeman's gun? You know my father's a reserve cop, right? I got his gun in my kitchen and would be glad to let you hold it. Just come in the house with me. Hurry."

Justin walked up the short driveway and entered the side door. The killer, a large, overweight, unkempt sixteen-year-old high school student was waiting for him by the kitchen counter wearing dirty work gloves.

"Where's the gun?" Justin asked.

"Over there by the sink behind the toaster," the burly killer said.

As Justin started walking toward the sink, the killer grabbed him from behind and stabbed him in his chest with a kitchen knife. Blood spilled over the kitchen floor as the helpless child slumped in his attacker's arms. The killer was careful not to let blood get on his own clothing as he gently placed Justin's body on the hard linoleum floor.

Working quickly, he wrapped Justin's limp body in several large garbage bags, carried it upstairs, and placed it on his bedroom floor. He ran downstairs and, using paper towels, old rags, and a wet mop, worked feverishly, thoroughly cleaning the blood off the kitchen floor. He sealed the used towels and rags and his work gloves in a black plastic bag, thinking he would put it in an outside rubbish barrel, knowing the rubbish man would make his weekly pickup early the next morning.

After carefully cleaning the murder weapon, he put it in his backpack, planning to bury it as soon as possible deep in the woods in an isolated part of town. He noticed blood spots on the front of his long sleeve shirt. Quickly, he tore off his shirt and put it in the plastic bag. He then rushed upstairs, put on a clean shirt and hid the body bag in the back of his bedroom closet, covering it as best he could under a pile of clothes and blankets. He hurriedly locked the closet door, deciding he would bury the body in the dirt floor in his cellar in the near future.

The consummate actor, he felt a rush of exhilaration reflecting on the scene he had just completed—the mysterious killer next door engaging in a bit of fun, whose meticulous planning and attention to detail made certain the police would never catch him.

Keeping the body in the house and then disposing of it was his only worry. With a watchdog grandmother and his elderly father and stepmother living downstairs, he had to be careful. He had to get the body out of his room and into the cellar very soon. Although his bedroom was his safe haven and off limits to other members of the household, he was afraid that someone might discover Justin's body if they inadvertently went looking for something in his room. Thank God he could lock his closet door and had the only key.

However, the cellar was clearly a better place for the body, a place none of the adults ever visited and where he spent many hours by himself writing on a discarded desk under a rusty old lamp. It was then that he remembered that there were two old trunks in a corner of the cellar where he could hide the body. He could dismember the body and wrap the body parts in blankets.

His initial thought of burying the body in the cellar now didn't make sense because there was more cement and little dirt space on the floor. It was better to get rid of the body parts over time when he was through with them. It would also allow him to keep a few lasting mementos of his perfect crime.

Although physically exhausted after dragging the body around his house, he had a commitment to keep. He was scheduled to sing at a folk Mass at St. Matthew's Church later that evening. If he changed his normal schedule, it might look suspicious later on. Besides, he never missed Mass on Sunday.

Chapter 3

George and Jane Doherty had moved to Massachusetts from Virginia with their three small children in 1971 and shortly thereafter purchased the house at 23 Suffork Street in Hopeville.

Hopeville at the time was a small, semi-rural community in the foothills of the Berkshires, many of whose approximately ten thousand residents were still struggling to rebound from the exodus of a large textile mill fifteen years before. The remnants of the old mill could be seen from a rotary in the center of town that was encircled by a number of gin mills, a liquor store, two restaurants, two barbershops, and a small strip mall. A low-income subsidized housing project and the Hopeville fire station extended down Center Street, a major road that connected Hopeville with the town of Greenfield. Springfield was the nearest city, about a forty-minute ride away.

Many dilapidated pre-World War II single and two story homes were situated on lazy streets that spread like tentacles up the small hills in the center of town. Visible in the distance was the rooftop bell tower of Hopeville High School, an austere red brick structure built in 1919, and St. Matthew's Catholic Church, its dark gothic exterior staring down on the busy traffic of Center Street.

A branch of the state college was situated in Hopeville, along with a regional hospital and small plastic companies that occupied a portion of the vacant mill space. Although several professors, lawyers, and doctors lived in town, the large majority of residents were hard working, blue-collar people who loved their town, enjoyed a unique sense of volunteerism, and felt Hopeville was a great place to raise their children. Life in Hopeville, they say, was as predictable as the tour buses that stopped at the town center restaurants every fall on their way to view the Vermont foliage, or the flood of families that rolled through the town in the winter months with skis fastened to their carracks.

George and Jane had met and married in Tennessee before living in Virginia for a short time and then migrating to Hopeville, where George planned to join the furniture business owned by his mom and dad. During their first few years there, he worked as a mechanic in a local garage by day and at night worked at the family store on Center Street. Jane was a "stay at home" mom and later took a part-time job as a school crossing guard.

They were an attractive couple in their mid-twenties. George was tall and slender with a ready grin and accompanying dimples while Jane was a petite, strawberry blond with a deep southern drawl that both fascinated and delighted her Yankee neighbors. Jane had a slight gap between her two front teeth just like her youngest son, Justin. In fact, blond-headed, freckled-faced, impish Justin was the spitting image of his mother.

Both George and his wife were strong disciplinarians, believing "If you spare the rod, you will spoil the child." Reflecting on his childhood, Joey Doherty described his parents as setting high behavioral standards that, "You darn well better follow or else. As kids we were given strict boundaries where we could go and not go in the neighborhood."

George also had a temper that struck fear into his children. "You never wanted to get my Dad angry," Joey explained. "Believe me, if you ever did anything dishonest, were outright disobedient or did something really wrong, you paid the price!"

Like many men with strong tempers, George feared saying and doing things in the heat of anger and on many occasions stepped back so that his wife could administer punishment to the children. This pattern of repressed anger continued in the years that followed the disappearance of Justin, as Jane became their spokesperson with the police and media.

One telling exchange occurred a few years after Justin disappeared. A hypnotist who lent his assistance to the case asked Jane, "Was Justin the type of youngster who was friendly and carefree, someone who would jump on his bike and ride around the neighborhood talking to just about anyone?"

"No way. Just the opposite," she said. "In 1975, Justin was the baby of the family while Joey was in kindergarten. So, Justin was the only one at home. He knew all the kids in the neighborhood, all the parents, sisters, brothers, aunts, the whole nine yards. However, he was so shy that when he went to his little friend Charlie Tracey's house, he wouldn't take orange juice from Charlie's mother. He wouldn't even take anything from his own grandparents unless I said it was all right.

"One time when he was five I left him in the car for two minutes as I ran into a store to drop off an item. I usually don't do that but it was getting to the point where I couldn't leave his side without his whining.

"I said to him, 'I want you to sit in the car. Mommy will come right back out.' Well, when I returned, he was screaming at the top of his lungs and crying for me. A lady was at the car asking him if he had lost his mother. I interrupted her in mid-sentence and said, 'No, he hasn't lost me yet.' You know what? A huge grin came on his face and the tears stopped."

It was now 6 p.m. and. Justin wasn't home yet. Nobody had seen him. He was late for dinner and Jane was starting to get alarmed. She asked George to check the housing project and, if necessary, drive around the neighborhood to find him and bring him home.

Chapter 4

George jumped into his remodeled fire-engine red, 1964 Ford sedan and drove around the neighborhood and housing project asking parents and others on the street if they had seen Justin. No one had. Something isn't right, George thought. This is so unlike Justin.

A sick feeling swelled in his stomach. He tried not to panic. There was some harmless reason why Justin was momentarily missing. He may have just wandered outside the immediate neighborhood.

He remembered that Justin and a young friend, without their parents' knowledge, had recently walked up the street to Saugus Pond, a popular fishing spot a mile north of Suffork Street. He and Jane had severely reprimanded Justin and told him never to go there ever again. George drove to the pond, got out of his car and walked around the water's edge. A slight mist had settled on the silky pond surface as a brilliant orange sun began to set on the yellow horizon. Although it was a tranquil scene, its silence seemed a bit eerie. He heard his voice echo as he called his son's name repeatedly, but no response came from his little Justin. Anxiety started to overcome him and he felt extremely lightheaded. "Did he drown? He has never been out of our sight by himself for any length of time. Something is wrong, very wrong."

When George returned home empty-handed, with no word on Justin's whereabouts, Jane saw the stark look of fear on her husband's face. "George, where is he?" she wailed. Justin's older brother, Joey and sister, Robin, suddenly stopped eating their supper and quietly lowered their heads. George started to sweat and was on the verge of vomiting. Jane looked on her husband's worried face and suddenly experienced a surge of dizziness, but thankfully managed to avoid fainting.

Neighbors immediately came to their home and rallied around the family, searching up and down Suffork and nearby streets. They phoned nearby friends throughout town to ask if they had seen Justin. They too came up empty. It was time to call the police.

Starting to panic, Jane hurriedly called the desk officer at the station, who recorded the following information:

"Jane Doherty of 23 Suffork Street has filed a report that her son, Justin, is missing. The last time he was seen was at 5 p.m. playing at the rear of the low-income housing project on Main Street. Justin is age five, six months, with blond hair, blue eyes and fair complexion. He is three feet tall, between forty and fifty pounds with a slim frame. He has a pockmark on the tip of his nose and a speech impediment. When last seen he was wearing a short-sleeved polo shirt and maroon trousers with a lion's patch on the right knee. Date of birth is 1-05-1970."

Little did anyone know that this description would appear frequently in newspapers and on television screens throughout the country for the next seven years.

The officer in charge called the fire chief, who requested that the rescue signal be sounded. This signal called all regular personnel, including fire and rescue volunteers, to report to the police station for the purpose of conducting a search for a missing child.

Chapter 5

Detective Captain Rick Thurston had just returned from a day at the stock car races in Connecticut when he received a call from the desk sergeant at the Hopeville police station.

"Rick, sorry to bother you. We have a missing child on 23 Suffork Street. Jane and George Doherty are the parents. Their five-year-old son, Justin, is missing. Stop by the station on your way to their house. I've typed up the boy's description given by the mother."

Thurston threw on his police jacket, "Okay. Do me a favor, call Harrison and tell him to meet me at the station in thirty minutes. I know he's home. We went to the races together and I left him at his house about an hour ago. See you at the station in fifteen minutes. Remember, call Harrison. Over and out."

Rick Thurston had been a Hopeville policeman for twenty-three years, working his way up to Detective Captain in charge of criminal investigations. He headed a unit consisting of three younger detectives—Chuck Harrison, Jeff Childs, and Harry Monroe.

He began his career in the 1950's when the town was much smaller, the police knew all the families, and as the old-timers say, "In those days, the cops cut you some slack." During the next twenty-four years, the town grew, and the personal relationship between townsfolk and the police dissipated with every new class of police recruits that joined the force.

Rick Thurston was an exception. He loved being a cop and, while on duty, took his job very seriously. Tall, with an athletic build and dark slicked-back hair, he was a handsome guy, and walked with a bit of a swagger. Friendly, with an upbeat sense of humor and a quick wit, he was what they called in Hopeville, "a real charmer." He was forty-three when Justin disappeared.

Some characterized him as being a bit on the wild side, off duty that is. He enjoyed partying into the late hours. He loved fast cars and he had wrecked several over the years, one time going off a local bridge late at night. He was particularly attracted to good-looking women, and they to him. He engaged everyone around him with his dashing personality and his self-deprecation in responding to pointed questions about his latest off duty escapade. As one of his friends said, "Rick is unique. They threw away the mold after the stork delivered him. You can't help but love the guy."

Rumors about Rick's meanderings were always circulating. Townspeople saw him as a cross between Errol Flynn, the swashbuckling actor who led a somewhat controversial off-screen life and the impeccably dressed, sympathetic police officer in the Norman Rockwell cover on the Saturday Evening Post. However, one thing was never questioned. When Rick put on his uniform, he was a committed, compassionate, and competent police officer.

Detective Sergeant Chuck Harrison was in his early thirties. Like Rick, his boss and buddy, he was a big, strapping, personable fellow, thoughtful and articulate, who had quickly moved through the police ranks to detective status. Chuck enjoyed the camaraderie that existed with Rick and the other detectives. The group was a close fraternity that socialized frequently, tipping a few beers during off duty hours in several local establishments.

A native of New Jersey, Chuck had been stationed in Boston while in the Navy and came to like the Berkshire area after visiting friends there on several occasions. Upon his discharge, he applied for a patrolman's vacancy in Hopeville and was surprised and delighted when, though an outsider, he actually got hired. In the late 1980's, Harrison retired from the force and returned to his native New Jersey, where he worked as a homicide investigator with the New Jersey Department of Justice.

The two men were indebted to long time Chief of Police Donald Sawyer for the opportunities he had given them to further their careers. Both attended the FBI Academy and other professional training programs throughout the country. Harrison also obtained his degree in criminal justice from the local college.

Thurston and Harrison were highly trained, experienced detectives in 1975. They were also about to face, the biggest challenge of their professional careers—a challenge that called for extraordinary patience, incredible energy, and the utmost competence.

Chapter 6

When Detectives Thurston and Harrison arrived at the Doherty home, an old gray mill house with black trim and a bright red front door, they found two distraught young parents sitting on the living room sofa, tightly clutching their two children. Thurston tried to put the family at ease by telling them that it was not unusual for a young boy to be missing for over two hours.

"Our procedure will be to fan out and question anyone who may have seen Justin. We'll look for clues and not take anything for granted. We'll ask neighbors to direct our search party to the boy's familiar territory, including Saugus Pond. Volunteers will thoroughly search not only Suffork Street but surrounding streets and woods as well. We'll find him. It is just a matter of time."

After talking with the family, the detectives immediately began a full-scale search. They searched the apartments in the low-income housing project where Justin and his friends had been playing. The Doherty property was searched several times. As fire engines, rescue vehicles, ambulances, and media types clogged the street, creating a collage of flashing red lights, Thurston and Harrison went door to door asking homeowners to check their houses, attics, cellars, garages, sheds, campers and outer buildings on their property.

As darkness set in, the searchers hadn't found Justin or received any clues to his whereabouts. No one had seen him in the surrounding streets, in the area of the pond, or in the town center. George, Jane, Robin, and Joey Doherty were unable to sleep that evening. For years after, the awful jolt they were given that day would cause many sleepless nights.

Thurston knew that in most missing child cases the first forty-eight hours were critical, something he didn't want to mention to the family. He knew he needed to act fast and call in reinforcements to help conduct a wider search. He contacted the head of the Massachusetts

State Police, who immediately assigned four state troopers to the case full-time. He asked the National Guard for their assistance and they granted it immediately.

On Monday morning, an all-out hunt began. As state helicopters painstakingly circled the area, the immediate focus was within a three-mile radius of Suffork Street.

The Hopeville and state police established temporary headquarters in the kitchen and dining room of local volunteer firefighter and Suffork Street resident, Todd Jenks, a jovial little man with piercing blue eyes and a shiny baldhead.

Jenks described the scene, "My house was a beehive of activity with local and state police and fire and rescue volunteers coming and going with radios and phones squawking everywhere. Donuts and coffee cups were all over my house. It was a real madhouse."

By Monday afternoon, volunteers responding to radio, television, and newspaper pleas started to arrive from as far away as Maine. The youngest were teenagers and the oldest in their seventies and eighties. Local high school students and area boy scouts skipped school and neighbors, local businessmen, and other townspeople stayed home from work to join the cadre of searchers.

The *Hopeville Times* reported the next day: "Houses, ponds, rivers, brooks, catch basins, vacant buildings, and heavily wooded and swampy areas were searched and searched again. By dawn on Monday, all available policemen and state troopers from every barracks supplemented the volunteers. Helicopters hovered, scuba divers dove, bloodhounds sniffed, and fire engines and ambulances flared. Questions were asked to everyone. But still no Justin."

Detectives Thurston and Harrison, joined by firemen, again went door to door on Suffork Street to see if owners had indeed searched their property completely.

Jenks explained his role in this phase of the search. "Although the houses on our street weren't searched, the cellars, sheds, and cesspools were searched by volunteer firemen. I know because I searched the cellar, garage, and shed of the Stedman house next door. Firemen or police, however, didn't search other parts of the houses. Only the Doherty house and the apartments in the low-income project were personally fully searched by the police and firemen."

Monday ended with great disappointment. Two days of searching had revealed no new information. As the days passed, the suspicion of foul play increased. Fear spread throughout the community. One Suffork mother, Gloria Richmond, was quoted as saying, "We fear for our little ones. There are about thirty of them on this street. No one can sleep."

Chapter 7

As the search party grew to nearly five hundred people on Tuesday and Wednesday, Thurston and his detectives established two command posts. Chief Sawyer had dragged himself out of his sickbed to oversee the search, but left Thurston fully in charge of operations.

One command post was established at a vacant gas station on Center Street and was headed by Detective Harry Monroe, a newly appointed detective known for his professionalism and attention to detail. Search teams of ten to twenty persons each were dispatched from this location. The other command post was at the police station, where Thurston and Harrison, ably assisted by state troopers, handled calls. It was hoped that the high profile given to the case would generate numerous tips from callers—tips that the police officers stationed at the command post would investigate immediately.

The search teams systematically combed about a dozen square miles of predominately wooded areas and waterways surrounding Suffork Street. Scuba divers and volunteers on canoes searched the ponds and lakes and volunteer firemen roamed the town in their vehicles looking for Justin or someone who may have seen him. The entire Hopeville community mustered incredible support, as hundreds braved unseasonable heat and humidity, trudging through swamps and dense briars to find some clue to the boy's disappearance.

Several volunteers suffered from heat exhaustion and were taken by ambulance to the hospital. Others had their eyes scraped by brush. One elderly Connecticut couple found themselves among the sooty remnants of a recent major fire. When they emerged from this area, they were so covered with brush and blackened by soot they were barely recognizable. One policeman reportedly crawled through a two hundred foot sewer pipe at the end of a neighboring street looking for little Justin.

On Tuesday night, George Doherty, choking back tears, took his own appeal to the airwaves, pleading for any information connected to his son's disappearance. "I want him back. I've got to have him back."

One volunteer who took a day out of work to participate in the search gave this account, "I answered an appeal made by the police for volunteers who were familiar with the areas surrounding Suffork Street. I showed up at the fire station with other volunteers like myself who grew up within a five-mile radius of the Doherty house.

"I later learned that the Hopeville police were officially in charge of the search, but I was confused and thought the state police were really in charge. I remember an impressive state police major giving us our marching orders. Boy, was he a forceful, hard-nosed guy! Rigidly standing there like a Marine drill sergeant in his gray blue uniform, wide brimmed hat, spit-polished boots, and black leather gloves, he yelled out our orders like we were a bunch of young, ignorant recruits in boot camp.

"I was assigned a section of town where as a child I had roamed through the woods and trails that were directly in back of my old house. Volunteers from out of town were assigned to teams with local guys like me showing them the way. Remember, this was the third day of the search after they had finished looking in the immediate area around Suffork Street.

"As I searched fruitlessly with my team through the rough terrain, I asked myself what are we doing? The boy is not in Hopeville! Someone has kidnapped him and taken him out of town. It's just a matter of time before the phone rings in the police station with a demand for ransom.

"He may have been accosted by a couple who plan on raising him as part of their family. If he still is in town, there is a real possibility that foul play has occurred. Don't the police know that most crimes of this nature occur within five hundred yards of the victim's house? I wonder how thoroughly they searched everyone's house. What are we doing stumbling through dense forests all over town?"

Not everyone agreed with the opinion of this brash volunteer, a crotchety "Townie."

Meanwhile, a core contingent of police, firemen, and volunteers persisted in their intense search, tramping through the dense woods and slippery swamps of Hopeville. Nonetheless, by the fifth day of the search the number of volunteers had dropped from a high of five hundred to one hundred fifty.

Chapter 8

The killer didn't join the search on Monday. He had other plans. Hamlet was playing in Stratford, Connecticut, and he had a ticket.

On Tuesday, he thought it might be a good idea to be seen—a little deception was in order. He lumbered up to St. Matthew's Cemetery and placed some bones in the woods between the cemetery and Saugus Pond.

When he walked to the gates outside the cemetery, he noticed that a crowd of volunteers had gathered to begin a search of the area. He heard the earth shaking thump-thump-thump of the state helicopter hovering above, preparing to land in front of the gates.

It was time for him to perform in the realistic drama he was cleverly crafting. Waving his hands wildly, he began signaling the pilot attempting to direct the plane's landing. Such exhibitionism was out of character for him, but in his newfound excitement he wanted to conceive, direct and act in his own production.

When the helicopter landed, a somber Thurston and three cocky state troopers in their impressive Mounties hats disembarked and began discussing ways of coordinating air and ground efforts in the area surrounding the pond and cemetery. Thurston had received a call from a psychic on Monday who insisted that she was certain that the boy disappeared near a body of water near his neighborhood and searching on and around Saugus Pond was now a priority.

The killer waited patiently until Thurston and the troopers finished their conversation and, twitching nervously, approached a nearby policeman to tell him he had been searching the area by himself and spotted some bones down by the shore of the pond. The policeman and several firemen followed him to the site where he had half-buried the bones. A short time later, tests revealed they were old dog bones.

As the focus of the search shifted from Suffork Street to other sections of town and people became more convinced that Justin had been kidnapped and taken out of town, he started to relax. He would never be caught. If he didn't make it as a great actor, maybe he could be a writer or director of plays like the real one that was now unfolding, a play that was totally his, not to be shared with anyone. He had complete control over this production.

Chapter 9

George and Jane Doherty participated in the search throughout, scarcely stopping to eat or sleep, but as it proceeded without yielding any results, their hopes began to dwindle.

Rick Thurston said to the press, "Let's face it. They're pretty down about this thing by now. They're exhausted, can't sleep, are worn out and impatient about finding their son, and we can't give them any encouragement other than saying we will just keep searching."

Jane Doherty's brittle emotional state got a severe jolt on Wednesday when she received a call from an unidentified woman with a husky voice who asked if George Doherty was at home. Jane said no and the caller replied, "I have your son and I am not giving him back." Jane's heart raced as she pleaded with the woman to tell her where she had Justin. "Call the Greenfield police, if you want the details" said the caller.

"Did you say the Greenfield police?"

"Yes," said the woman. Jane pressed for more information, but the woman abruptly hung up. With the phone cord and receiver dangling from her clenched fist, Jane stood paralyzed for several minutes before breaking into sobs.

A short time later, the woman called again asking for Jane, but, as the police had instructed, Jane limited the conversation by slowly saying, "I have another phone call and can't talk to you now." Fortunately, the state police had installed a tape recorder soon after Justin had disappeared on Sunday, so both conversations were taped.

The woman was identified as a twenty-nine-year-old Greenfield resident. She was arrested at her home and charged with making harassing phone calls to the Doherty home. After first lying about the details of the phone conversation, she admitted to making the calls, claiming she was just trying to help. What she said made little sense. "I thought I could be of some assistance because I had a friend whose little boy was missing but later found, so I know how the Doherty family feels."

The woman was held at a state health clinic in Springfield. After her arraignment, she pleaded innocent through her lawyer, who told the court that his client had been under treatment at the health clinic for some time.

The newspaper reported that Thurston, his detectives, and state police traced forty-five leads at the command center during the first week of the search. According to Thurston, "Calls were coming in from all over. Everyone had a theory about what might have happened to Justin or saw something or someone who looked suspicious. I felt like an exhausted ringmaster in a traveling circus that had too many animal acts to handle at one time."

By about the third day of the search, the crazies came out of the woodwork—astrologists, psychics, and hypnotists among others. Though some were sincerely attempting to help, some just wanted their names in the paper, and others were mostly interested in the reward money being offered for information,

Harrison considered many of these people distractions. "This was our first real high profile case and the largest state manhunt ever conducted by a small town police department. We talked to everyone and followed up on every call and I privately questioned the wisdom in doing that. We wasted too much time and effort. We should have asked callers to put their information in writing, allowing us to paper screen and then decide exactly what to follow up on."

Upon hearing Harrison's opinion, Police Chief Sawyer chuckled, saying, "Yeah, hindsight is always twenty-twenty, but Chuck Harrison has a point. I remember the state police major assigned to our case saying to me after he had taken several strange calls from some locals, 'God, you have some pretty weird people living in this town.'"

Chapter 10

By Thursday, Detective Captain Rick Thurston was getting frustrated. The leads he had received were going nowhere.

The police had learned that an older man with a child resembling Justin was seen boarding a bus to Springfield. The bus driver, when he was located and shown a picture of the missing boy, believed the child could have been Justin. With the help of Springfield police, the elderly man was tracked down. He told the police that he had been in Hopeville with his blond haired, five-year-old granddaughter to leave his car off for repairs and then took a bus back to Springfield. His story checked out. Again, just another dead end.

One emotional woman with a raspy voice called claiming she had heard one of the older boys in the housing project say he would split Justin's head open and put him in a wooden box. The police interviewed the boy and his mother, but nothing useful came of this report as well.

Thurston talked with a Center Street resident who reported seeing a strange, pock-faced man with a dyed-green ponytail hanging around the Wayside Bar. He claimed he was a faith healer who had information about Justin's disappearance. This lead also failed to develop; the man was just another homeless person drifting through Hopeville.

A twelve-year-old girl reported what sounded like a promising lead. She claimed she saw a man supposedly named David pick up a boy on Center Street in a blue car. Earlier, an older woman had also reported the name "David" to the police as a person who had a history of child molestation and should be checked out. When interviewed, the shy and highly nervous young girl admitted to fabricating the story. The only David she knew was a handicapped boy in the sixth grade that was too young to have a license and had never driven a car.

The police then contacted the woman in her late eighties who had called regarding David and learned she was confined to a wheelchair.

After a long period of questioning, the police finally learned the correct name of the suspect. He was a chunky, fair skinned sixteen-year-old boy from a neighboring town who had been appearing at the search sites throughout the week. The boy and the older woman were given polygraph tests with clean results. He had no history of child molestation. Apparently, he was a distant relative of hers who she despised for some unknown reason.

The detectives processed these leads and others, but no solid clues to Justin's disappearance surfaced. A humble Thurston told the local papers, "We're totally baffled and haven't turned up one shred of evidence since we started this search on Sunday."

When pressed by the state and local media, he added, "If foul play is involved, kidnapping for ransom appears to be unlikely because the family does not have much money. We can't come up with a motive. Of course, there is always the fear that some nut picked him up."

Thurston struggled over the decision to call off the search, remembering his promise to George and Jane Doherty. "We'll do everything we can to find the little guy," he had told them as he looked into Jane's sorrowful eyes and saw the tortuous pain spread across her tired, drawn face.

By Thursday evening Thurston knew he had to make a decision. The search had been in process for four days. It was time either to call it off or start over again, redoubling the effort. He decided to mount a massive search of the entire twenty-six square miles of Hopeville. The current search would stop on Friday afternoon, to allow the searchers a brief rest. He would ask people from Massachusetts and neighboring states to join a large-scale search for Justin on Saturday and Sunday. As he prepared his statement for the press, he appealed to the public, "Please keep calling in tips. Nobody, nothing sounds foolish. I don't want anybody to become so discouraged they won't call us if they think of something. Please join us as we conduct a massive search for little Justin."

He and his detectives had to organize quickly; this would be the biggest search ever conducted in all of New England.

Thurston wondered if he might be over his head. He got little sleep Friday night. He woke up several times in a cold sweat; feeling like someone was pounding the side of his skull with their bare knuckles. He knew his reputation was at stake. He didn't want to be remembered as the local cop who led hordes of people on a wild goose chase.

Chapter 11

Detective Harry Monroe was a Hopeville cop well respected for his organizational skills and extensive knowledge of the town's topography. A former athlete at Hopeville High School with good looks and wavy blond hair, he could have modeled for physical fitness magazine covers. Harry was foremost a serious minded family man in his early thirties who had a son the same age as Justin.

Harry was initially responsible for setting up the command center at the vacant service station and plotting the search areas on a map of the town. His command center also transported the searchers to the designated search areas in town and handled all communications in the field with rescue and fire units. He established a kitchen at the command center where the searchers were fed a light breakfast, a box lunch, and dinner. Local organizations such as schools and churches supplied most of the food, and appeals were made to volunteers to assist in preparing sandwiches and hot meals.

With so little time to organize a search of this magnitude, Harry and other planners were up until midnight Friday planning a strategy and were ready to see if it would work. One spirited coordinator at the command center commented, "We're going to give it a damned good try. We've got the town blanketed."

With a potentially fifteen hundred searchers invading the town on Saturday, Harry knew he had to make some major changes in his operation. He decided to establish three command posts. The chief command center was established at the local state college parking lot, with Harry and several patrolmen operating out of a mobile trailer. All volunteers were asked to wear appropriate clothing and report to this location, where they would be organized, fed, and receive their search assignments.

Starting at 7 a.m. on Saturday, volunteers filtered in wearing jeans, fatigues, boots, sneakers, headbands, long shirts, short shirts, and carrying walking sticks and machetes. They were told to walk "Arm in arm, with the slowest person setting the pace," and to "Check every bush; leave nothing out. Don't just look at the ground. There are trees where he could have climbed."

Volunteers were assembled into groups of forty, each with at least one "walkie- talkie" and a radio monitor to record progress, and transported by school buses to twenty-five different search locations within the town.

The second command center remained at the vacant gas station where sixty state troopers once again gathered to go door to door in the boy's immediate neighborhood interviewing homeowners and their families.

The third command post was established at the local junior high school parking lot and consisted of a mounting fleet of fire and rescue units from area communities whose purpose was to cover the town's waterways. Todd Jenks now had his kitchen back since law enforcement officials no longer needed his house as a meeting place.

National Guard and Marine units from Boston and Springfield and other rescue units from Rhode Island and Massachusetts joined the search. Citizens band radio units from Rhode Island, Connecticut, and Massachusetts kept searchers in touch with command posts ably run by a zany but dedicated local radio group called the Cotton Pickin' Bandits.

Saugus Pond was drained to a level where corporate, National Guard, and state helicopters could see the bottom. Four wheel drive vehicle and motorcycle units covered back trails and swamp areas; every body of water was combed by boats and divers; backhoes were used to dig up caves; storm drains and well and cesspool openings were re-checked. Meanwhile, the noisy helicopters continued flying in predetermined patterns over the town during the massive two-day effort.

Interviews by local and area newspaper reporters revealed that the volunteers came from all over New England in different sizes, shapes, and ages, from groups of high school students to senior citizens. They made comments like, "I was going to the beach today but my conscience wouldn't let me. Good Lord, I'd rather find that child one way or another than have his parents worry forever."

Another volunteer said, "I feel so badly for the parents. I have the feeling I don't want to be the one to find the boy if the worst happened. It's tough to say. You hope you do and you hope you don't."

With little to show for their efforts as Saturday ended, many of the dedicated searchers declared, "I'll be back tomorrow" and indeed they did return in force.

Detective Monroe, as search field coordinator, carefully plotted the square miles and areas of the town. He estimated that the twenty-six square miles of the town had been covered. His town map recordings crossed frequently, indicating that several key areas had been searched more than once. He also estimated that over the two days approximately twelve hundred volunteers participated in the search despite temperatures that reached into the nineties.

As the search ended Sunday, newspapers reported that the searchers had been told by the police at the outset, "No job we have is unimportant; and in these two days every little thing found could be important."

But at the end there was no Justin. The only items found—pants, shoes, shirts, sneakers and toys—all were determined by the police to be unrelated to Justin's disappearance.

Chapter 12

Although the search ended on Sunday night, a small steadfast group of volunteers refused to quit, and again gathered at the college parking lot on Monday morning ready for duty.

Rick Thurston and Harry Monroe were in a quandary. Who is going to tell them that the search is over and send them home? The two detectives tossed this question back and forth. "You break the bad news, Captain," Monroe said.

"No way, Harry, no way," Thurston shot back. "If I do it I will have a revolt on my hands."

Eventually, both detectives agreed to share the task of telling the volunteers it was over. The two men were teary-eyed as they looked at the weary faces of the volunteers. They spoke softly and with deep emotion. It was very difficult for them to deliver the bad news, but they felt they had no choice.

After hearing the news, the volunteers stood motionless. Several shouted, "You can't stop now! Give it another couple of days!" It was clear the devoted searchers were so closely bonded after days of walking together through dense woods in suffocating heat to help find some helpful evidence that they would not quit. In fact, several felt so strongly that they didn't quit that day. They insisted that certain key areas in the town needed to be rechecked and continued searching on their own for most of that Monday.

In the meantime, Thurston publicly announced, "Although the formal search is over, we will actively continue our investigation. The Doherty family and the police department have not given up hope that the boy will be found. Although the search gave us nothing to go on, the search is far from dead." His official sounding pronouncement hid his bitter disappointment. He had come up empty.

But the fruitless search had accomplished one thing. It had convinced the police that someone must have taken the boy and left town. The hope that Thurston referred to arose from the likelihood that Justin had been seized by someone, probably a couple, and taken out of town or even out of state. Understandably, Jane wanted to believe that her son was still alive and living with some other family. In the torturous years that followed, she never gave up hope of that possibility.

Unfortunately, the search swung the investigation in the wrong direction, away from neighborhoods of Hopeville to other cities in Massachusetts, border states and various locations throughout the country. The possibility that Justin might have been killed by a Hopeville native who kept the boy's dead body in his house apparently never occurred to the investigators. If it did, it surely never received serious attention.

However, the prolonged, arduous search did have a remarkable effect on the good people of Hopeville. The search was a time when caring people in a community came together like never before. They held hands with their neighbors and helping strangers, they prayed together, and they bravely fought heat exhaustion and lack of sleep for a common cause, one that touched their very souls.

In the next weekly edition of the *Hopeville Times*, an editorial beautifully captured what happened during that memorable experience shared by so many:

It is obvious that in this space, this week, words should be written to bring into focus what has happened here since Justin Doherty, age five, was insanely plucked into oblivion a week ago Sunday.

"But the story of Justin, and whatever has happened to him, does not permit that close an examination. Something stirs in the pit of the stomach that warns one of profound, grievous fears lying inside, marrow-deep and best left undisturbed for peace of mind.

"What happened to Justin is every person's nightmare come true, and it conjures up twin specters which are equally difficult to face. We are compassionate because he was so young, and so radiant, and at age five, such pitifully easy prey for fortune or fortune hunter.

"And we who are children, parents and grandparents must face the cold, blunt edge of reality telling us that we, and ours, are as susceptible to the same as Justin and his.

"So to tell the story of Justin it is necessary to look elsewhere and to

talk about what people do when such things happen—at least what they do around here.

"To belabor the colossal effort of last week would be unthinkable, in light of existing circumstances. But to ignore it would be an injustice as well. The output in terms of energy, determination, money, time, food, supplies, and most of all – concern was enormous. The individuals involved, from policemen, to neighbors, to out-of-towners who came because a child was lost, know who they are, and need no personal thanks.

"Some were strong and tireless, and others fell from exhaustion, cuts and bruises, themselves becoming casualties in this bizarre, heartbreaking incident.

"It cannot be said that Hopeville did not weep for Justin, but it did so with the realization that methodical, bone-wearying labor, and not handwringing, was the only chance it had.

"Any hint of victory, or even accomplishment, turns immediately to ashes in view of what has happened so far. But for Justin, an awful lot of people did the very best they could."

Chapter 13

At five o'clock Mass, the popular Christian folk group began singing "On Eagles Wings." Much to his chagrin, Norman Stedman was only a back-up singer. Although he got along well with members of the group and never missed a Mass, he was disappointed that no one appreciated his singing. They were nice enough people, but blind when it came to recognizing talent. He was convinced he could do a much better job than the whimpering lead singer.

After the song, Norman lapsed into a deep trance. He was shaking lately and was concerned that people would notice that he was more nervous than usual. He was relieved that the search was over. Yes, the police got close but they were no match for him. In fact, executing his perfect crime had been especially exciting.

After the search ended, he had carried Justin's dead body from his bedroom into his cellar where he put it in an old wooden trunk and covered it with a ragged comforter.

Norman knew he had to do something with the body before it started to decompose. He had to act quickly. Although its stench would be somewhat absorbed by blankets and thought to be the rotten stench already in the house caused by animal odor and filthy litter, he was afraid that any increase in the intensity of the present house smell might lead to the discovery of the dead body by visitors or other family members. He had to act fast.

Consequently, he worked feverishly in his cellar dismembering the body and placing the pieces in cloth bags that fit nicely into his large backpack. Over the next few weeks, he accompanied his father on his weekly "dump picking" trips to the town landfill, where he discreetly got out of the truck and disposed of the small body bags.

The remaining body parts he kept in the trunk in the cellar, trying to decide what to do with them. He had read about ways to boil the flesh off the bones of a dead animal, but needed to research the best chemical solution to use. Eventually, he decided to boil the body parts in a weak lye solution and was pleased when the flesh slid cleanly off the bones.

After he had stripped the remaining bones, he took them out of the cellar trunk and hid them in his bedroom closet, with one exception; he kept Justin's skull in a box on his dresser as a reminder of his greatest theatrical performance to date.

Chapter 14

"Jane Doherty was an amazing woman," Thurston explained. "I really admired her."

He told her everything he knew and she kept him informed of every telephone call and piece of correspondence, good or bad, she received regarding the case. She was a fighter, and although difficult for her, she managed to keep a cheerful smile on her face through some very trying times.

After the search failed to provide any clues to Justin's disappearance, Jane began a personal campaign to find her son. She mailed hundreds of fliers containing his picture and vital statistics to newspapers and police departments throughout the country. She contacted national magazines and tabloid newspapers asking for their help. She contacted John Walsh who later produced *America's Most Wanted* television show for his assistance. Never succumbing to depression and self-pity, she somehow summoned more energy than she ever had before to lead a personal crusade to find her son.

When asked at this point in the case if he had given up hope that Justin was still alive, Rick Thurston insisted that he believed they would find the boy—it would just take time. When asked whether the boy would be found dead or alive, he was unresponsive.

George Doherty reacted differently to the failed search. He didn't want to discuss the case with anyone, and while Jane pushed to keep public awareness of the crime alive, he seemed to withdraw and became very introspective.

According to Chief Sawyer and Thurston, they rarely saw George and never talked to him about the on-going investigation. Always private, he repressed the painful thoughts of what might have happened to his son, along with an increasing anger with the police department's failure to find Justin or uncover any real clues to his whereabouts. He feared losing control of his emotions and doing and saying something to embarrass his family. As a result, Jane became both the primary family spokesperson and the tireless activist who would stop at nothing to find Justin.

State police remained at the Hopeville Police Station for a few weeks after the search, helping the local force screen the flood of incoming phone calls. Practically everyone had a lead to report, a story to tell, an opinion or a prayer to offer, or expertise as a psychic, hypnotist, healer, or astrologist to share.

For seven years, the letters and phone calls never stopped coming as the Hopeville police kept the case active. For example, a Hopeville man who was coon hunting by Saugus Pond called the police to say that he detected an awful smell coming from a sandy beach. Police officers checked the area and dug up a dead snapping turtle.

After making an elaborate chart, an astrologist wrote, "I don't think he is alive, but he will be found before the first anniversary of this disappearance."

A psychic from San Francisco wrote, "Be on the lookout for someone who talks with his hands." This, of course, pertained to about everyone in town.

A Springfield man called the police and said he was a fully disabled Korean War veteran and had psychic powers. He told the police that the boy's body was buried in a cellar in the neighborhood. When detectives questioned his live-in boyfriend he said, "When my friend drinks too much, he does stupid things." Time would prove that this war vet was, surprisingly, right on target.

The most damaging call came from an unknown party who claimed that Jane and George beat Justin on several occasions and that Justin might be in the custody of someone in the immediate family. The caller also implied that the parents might have murdered him. Unfortunately, this vicious rumor quickly spread throughout the town and added to the parents' torment. In total, the police subjected over one hundred people to polygraph tests during their investigation, and the first were George and Jane Doherty.

Detectives contacted the local postmaster and received a list of persons who had recently left Hopeville. They again conducted interviews with the people who had last seen Justin on that Sunday afternoon. No clues materialized.

A letter from Urbana, Illinois, indicated the name, license, and address of a kidnapper in Urbana who had recently been in Massachusetts. Upon checking, no one of the name given or a Justin Doherty had ever lived there.

The Worcester police received an intriguing call. Apparently, a patient from the University of Massachusetts Medical Center was seen in the Hopeville area at the time of the abduction. He had recently been arrested for fondling a young boy in Worcester. This lead evaporated when the police discovered that the man didn't read newspapers because he was illiterate, didn't drive, and would commit his indecent acts by befriending unsuspecting parents rather than riding around and picking up children.

Advice on how to proceed with the investigation came from numerous people. Two letters sent to Jane suggested that abductors could be part of a traveling circus that was currently appearing in a neighboring community. One lady wrote, "The police should check with the members of the circus to see if there is a couple missing. The possibilities are they might have the child. I hope that your son will be found shortly." After checking with circus officials, detectives dismissed that possibility.

A woman called and said she had seen a bearded older man in a blue Ford sedan pick up a young boy in front of Hopeville Fire Station that Sunday afternoon. The state police located the man and gave him a polygraph test. He was scared, knowing that the polygraph machine would record significant emotional disturbances if he admitted picking up even one boy, so he made up a story about picking up four or five boys, one of them being Justin, when he was shown Justin's photo. He said that he took the boys to a wooded area and left them there. When the polygraph indicated deception, the man confessed that he had picked up another boy, not Justin, but claimed he did not have sex with him. Upon investigation, the suspect's story checked out in all ways but one; he was subsequently charged with the sexual assault of the boy he had lured into his car and was found guilty.

Rick Thurston privately admitted that he was skeptical of the wackier information he received, particularly from astrologists and psychics. Jane, however, welcomed any advice. She and her daughter Robin even welcomed the assistance provided by hypnotists, as long as they were interested in helping her find Justin. Thurston diligently saw to it that every letter or call was checked out. He had promised Jane he would do that for her and he kept his promise.

Chapter 15

Thurston was once asked what he considered the best leads he had received during the years following the search.

He said, "We had a number of leads that looked promising. Myself, Monroe and Harrison followed up on several leads in various parts of the country. For example, we checked out a group in Putney, Vermont, that allegedly had kidnapped young kids, brought them deep into the woods, and later put them up for adoption. That lead never panned out.

"We received calls from several elementary school principals who indicated that new families with curious backgrounds had just moved into town and had sons who fit the description of Justin. Monroe and I actually took trips to schools in New York and New Jersey to trace down a couple of tips. One photo forwarded to us by a principal in Paterson, New Jersey, looked very much like Justin. Unfortunately, when we visited the school, it wasn't Justin; however, the resemblance was remarkable.

"One of the better leads we had concerned the Moon ministers, right here in Hopeville. In the 1970's, the Moonies were actively recruiting young people for the Unification Church headed by Revered Sun Myung Moon, who called himself the new Messiah, claiming Korea was God's chosen nation. Scores of parents were legally attempting to free their kids from what they claimed was brainwashing by Moon's ministers. Moon trained his ministers to preach the concepts of love and fraternity in order to have new recruits surrender control of their lives to Moon's church and his religious beliefs."

At first, Chief Sawyer was skeptical and asked Thurston why he thought the Moonies would seize someone like Justin, especially at his tender age.

He told the chief that he had received a lead from a reliable source that suggested he investigate whether the Moonies were in any way involved in the boy's disappearance. In fact, several Moonies were living in a house on Route 106 in Hopeville next to Sutton's oil company. They were selling Virginia peanuts in the town center and outside of stores and other business establishments in surrounding towns.

Thurston explained, "With the chief's permission, Chuck Harrison and I took a trip to Cooperstown, New York, where Revered Moon was headquartered. We went to his place and there were armed guards at the door. Big tough looking guys too. We tried to sneak in, but were unsuccessful. We later learned that the lead was a bogus one. We were disappointed, because we thought we were really on to something.

"At another time, we talked to a woman who claimed she had a vision on the night that Justin disappeared, claiming that she saw a trailer truck carrying cars with Justin inside the cab looking down at her. She gave an incredible detailed description of the boy and the truck; however, it was just another dead end.

"We also gave key suspects polygraph tests in another open murder case we have in our files. It occurred in 1968, when a young woman was found dead on the side of Briar Road.

"She was staying at her family's lake house in Greenfield and was last seen shopping at a convenience store on Center Street.

"This case is still open after all these years, although we do have suspects, one of whom we feel is the killer. We simply lack sufficient evidence to make an arrest. Because the body was quite decomposed when we found it, we have been unable to determine the exact cause of death. This blocks our attempt to make an arrest."

Shortly after Justin's disappearance, the Doherty family moved out of their house on Suffork Street to a larger house about a mile away on Center Street, directly across from St. Matthew's Church.

One neighbor felt that it was George's idea to move, "George wanted to move away from the bad memories in the Suffork Street house. He needed a change of scenery even though he and Jane were leaving good friends in the neighborhood. Justin's disappearance left a deep scar in George's heart and he needed to flee from any reminder of the terrible tragedy that now haunted him. Jane really didn't want to leave, but she understood George's feelings and went along with his wishes. Before they left, the family planted a peach tree on their front lawn in memory of Justin."

Chapter 16

Thurston finally received a lead that gave him and Jane Doherty some real hope.

Between June 1974 and September 1975, two other boys about the same age as Justin had also vanished into thin air. The boys lived in New England and may have been abducted. All attempts to find them, including a military detector jet and help from famed psychic Jeane Dixon were unsuccessful. Thurston thought that Justin's disappearance could be linked to these cases.

In the 1970's, technology with sophisticated computer data banks and advanced communications systems were only in the conceptual stage. Police departments were mainly connected to each other and with the FBI in Washington through Teletype. Thurston had learned about the two missing New England boys through Teletype transmissions with police in the two towns where they had disappeared.

Thurston shared the following information he received with his fellow detectives:

"The first boy was five-year-old David Louison, the son of one of the leading criminal lawyers in Massachusetts. David vanished in June 1974 while playing at a construction site near his home in Brockton, Massachusetts.

"The boy's father told the media of how horrible and painful the loss of their son was for his wife, who refused to discuss the case with anyone. To make matters worse, one caller said he knew the man who kidnapped the boy, but that he was a frightened person who had been a patient at a veterans' hospital in Massachusetts and needed help. David's father wrote two letters to the caller, but the man's claim was baseless. Two other men also separately claimed they had kidnapped David. They were arrested and prosecuted for extortion.

"David was never found. The parents donated the reward money for finding him to help establish a shelter for homeless families in Brockton.

"The second boy was four-year-old Kurt Newton, reported missing on Labor Day, 1975, at a campground in the dense woods of Chain of Ponds, Maine, just six miles from the Canadian border. His family, who was spending the weekend there, left him for ten minutes to play with several boys. The boys rode their Big Wheels down a dirt road and Kurt wandered away. His mother told the local paper, 'Someone took him. They could have easily taken him by boat across the lake by the campground and into Canada.'

"Although Kurt was a year younger, he also had blond hair and blue eyes and his height and weight matched Justin's. He's still missing."

As they had in Justin Doherty's case, Thurston indicated that police searched the areas where the boys disappeared with the help of hundreds of volunteers, printed up thousands of "missing posters" and interviewed neighbors and suspects with polygraph machines. Aircraft were also used in the two searches.

Thurston thought it plausible that Justin's disappearance might be connected to the other kidnappings. He got excited when, after contacting Brockton police, he learned that one of their prime suspects had a car registered to a man in neighboring Greenfield. Thurston and Harry Monroe immediately drove to Brockton to meet with the lead investigator in the case, John Orbone, a heavy-set, stern man in his fifties who had been a homicide detective for nearly twenty-five years. A long, unsightly scar running down the left side of his face reportedly received in a hand-to-hand fight with a group of gang members reminded everyone who met him that his was a dangerous job. Orbone was extremely helpful and allowed the two Hopeville detectives to run polygraph tests on a number of suspects.

When they talked with the suspect that had been driving the car registered to a Greenfield resident, they learned he was from Alabama and had a long criminal record. He had been charged with the sexual molestation of young boys several times, but never convicted. A grubby guy in his early forties with a pockmarked face and yellow-stained teeth, he claimed he had borrowed the car from his cousin in Greenfield and swore he had never been in Hopeville in his life.

The polygraph tests given to him and his cousin and a check with the Registry of Motor Vehicles revealed he was telling the truth. The two disappointed Hopeville detectives once again headed for home empty handed.

Chapter 17

"Of all the leads we received in the years of our continuing investigation," explained Thurston, "the one in Waterloo, New York, was by far the best. It was connected to Justin's disappearance in so many ways that I thought we finally had the guy."

"I was sitting in my office one day when I got a call from the Waterloo Chief of Police. He told me that he had arrested a guy for sexual assault and while they were booking him, he said, 'I had nothing to do with the Justin Doherty kidnapping.' The guy was a known sex molester who had admitted to molesting young children. He had been a suspect in a number of missing child cases and had previously lived in Worcester. His name always seemed to come up when there was a missing child case in New England."

Thurston and Chuck Harrison wasted no time in flying to Waterloo to meet with the local detectives and interview this "hot" suspect.

"When we got there the chief took us into the interrogation room where we saw this fat blob of a guy with a smug look on his face," Thurston explained.

"You knew he had been in this type of situation before. He was about forty-five, pasty white complexion, and had beady little green eyes. The chief hated this guy for good reason. He was arrested for sexually assaulting a son of one of his police officers a few weeks before. The chief's nephew had also been sexually assaulted in the recent past by another molester. The trooper in charge of the local barracks and the chief were so worked up that they started working this guy over in front of us. We told them we wanted none of that and they finally calmed down."

Chuck Harrison gave this account of their meeting with the suspect: "This weirdo was scary. We listened to audiotapes he had made and looked at photos he had taken of young children. The pictures of the kids were posted on the inside of an old bread truck he had. He would ride around town in the truck, watching and taking pictures of children on the playgrounds and in parks.

"He was mainly interested in young boys and would record on tape what he would do sexually to these kids when he cornered them. We learned that he was a prime suspect in a number of missing child cases. In fact, a few years ago in *People Magazine* there was an article about old, unsolved missing child cases that had occurred from California to Maine, and believe it or not, this guy's name was still listed as a prime suspect in a Massachusetts missing child case that occurred twenty years before. The authorities tried hard to put this guy away for years, but they have been unable to prosecute him for a serious crime. Unfortunately, he is still out there driving around."

Thurston added, "I'll tell you another thing. When you listen to those tapes, this guy had the creepiest, high-pitched voice you can ever imagine. Really eerie. It was much different than the voice we heard when we interviewed him. I can tell you that when I got home, I had difficulty seeing my kids get on the bus and go off to school. Both Chuck and I didn't realize there were such sick puppies out there preying on innocent kids.

"This is the guy who had been observed placing a cross on a small grave near a sewer project one time. The police thought that he buried a child there. They dug up the area, but found nothing. God, it was awful talking to this nut."

"Here is another unbelievable thing about this fellow," Harrison said. "When he lived in Worcester, he was active in the Boy Scouts and one year received an award for being the most outstanding scoutmaster in the state."

Thurston mentioned another thing that happened while he and Harrison were in Waterloo. "We surprisingly ran into Harold Gallagher at a local Italian restaurant. Harold was one of the state troopers who worked the Doherty case with us. He was taking his son back to college and offered to assist us in our investigation of this guy. He called his office in Boston and talked to his boss who told him to stay right there and provide us with any assistance we needed."

Even with Gallagher's help and the resources provided by the Waterloo Chief of Police and two state police offices in New York and Massachusetts, the most promising lead to date fizzled out. Thurston and Harrison were back to square one.

Chapter 18

Sometimes the private research of ordinary concerned citizens uncovers important facts not apparent to law enforcement officials. Many times, the authorities resent this intrusion and view these "busybodies" as a distraction. Such was the case of Karen Trasity.

A lengthy article appeared in the *Hopeville Times* about Karen, a thirty-five-year-old Springfield mother of two who had organized a group to investigate, educate, and lobby for the benefit of missing and abused children.

She had joined the search for Justin in Hopeville, but her interest and efforts didn't stop there. She conducted background research on several men arrested for child molesting and rape and relentlessly lobbied state officials, insisting that such persons should not be released on parole or sent to a mental institution. She believed that by the time sexual predators had committed their crimes it was too late for psychoanalysis to rehabilitate them.

"Let them see what it's like to be punished," was her mantra.

Karen Trasity developed her own theories on unsolved missing children crimes. She postulated that Justin and the two other missing boys from Massachusetts and Maine were part of a pattern of disappearances in New England since 1971. In addition to them, a number of girls also disappeared in the same time period and were later found dead.

She compiled very impressive statistics and argued that this number of missing children in a small region of the country during such a compressed time frame meant it was likely that the boys were still alive, perhaps together in a group. Her extensive work helped to sustain Jane and Thurston in their hopes that Justin was still alive.

While Karen constantly provided leads to police at her own expense, these met with mixed reviews. The state police were quoted in the paper as referring to her amateur sleuthing as, "annoying and suspect." But this small, feisty, red-haired wife of a firefighter would not be deterred. She took courses that led to a detective's license and a badge from the City of Springfield and started actively investigating cases on her own, regardless of the criticisms aimed at her by crime enforcement officials.

Thurston was an exception; he appreciated her research. "Mrs. Trasity came up with a lot of ideas worth following. I consider her efforts very sincere."

Karen appreciated his endorsement, "Detective Thurston followed up on every lead I gave him. Although none of the leads were fruitful, he never complained. And I sent him on some pretty wild goose chases too."

She and her budding organization were particularly bothered that no national or state information centers existed to categorize missing person cases. Her group's immediate goal was to compile a data bank that parents and police could easily access. Karen Trasity was indeed ahead of her time, but few people realized it.

When a newspaper reporter asked her why she was doing all that she was, she gave an answer that, perhaps unwittingly, defined the Doherty's and the detectives' dilemma,

"I don't know it's like being in the middle of a story without an ending."

Chapter 19

Rick Thurston and Jane Doherty didn't turn away hypnotists either.

Two South Boston residents, Irma Shelton and Ted Lyons, two self-appointed "investigative hypnotists" who had worked together on a number of unsolved cases, suddenly appeared one day in Hopeville and offered Jane Doherty their assistance.

Jane quickly accepted.

Irma was a sweet old lady in her late seventies with a dyed auburn coiffure, light reddish eyebrows, and a heavy spread of mascara that accentuated her sparse eyelashes and deep blue eyes. She spoke softly with a delightful Irish brogue.

Ted was a fast-talking, pudgy Irishman in his early fifties, reputed to be one of the most skillful and accomplished hypnotists in New England. He had a large following and appeared frequently in theaters and on television.

Ted and Irma's first move was to interview Jane and Robin Doherty. From the questions they asked, it was obvious they had done some preliminary research on Justin's disappearance prior to showing up on Jane's doorstep.

In his practiced, soothing tone, Ted began the interview:

Ted: Jane, where do you live on Suffork Street?

Jane: The fourth house as you go up the road.

Irma: I heard there was some psychic that thought Justin was in a lake?

Ted: Was that Saugus Pond?

Jane: Yes, they drained it.

Irma: They drained the pond?

Jane: They drained the pond and checked all the waterways and everything. They checked the woods going shoulder to shoulder or at arms length. My husband was out there every day in the middle of the search. They even brought out the bloodhounds.

Ted: Did they go through all the woods by the cemetery?

Jane: They went through the whole area. There wasn't a stone unturned. They checked all the waterways, septic tanks, wells, and the Mill complex. They checked everything.

After Jane's initial responses, Ted and Irma asked Robin questions about strange or suspicious characters she might have seen hanging around the Wayside Bar or in the immediate neighborhood. They also asked mother and daughter about dreams they might have had in which they had clear visions of Justin. They were interested in getting detailed descriptions of the dreams since any of Jane and Robin's visions could have value later on during hypnosis. Jane then shared her dreams.

Jane: I got up, now this is in my sleep, and went out the house and down the street and there was Justin.

Robin: I had dreams like that.

Jane: Now all my dreams never said anything about death. I had two I remember.

Ted: When were these dreams?

Jane: The first one was about a month after Justin disappeared. The dream took place in a farmhouse, a log type house and barn surrounded by fields.

Ted: What type of day was it?

Jane: I don't know.

Ted: Do you feel it was a bright, sunny day?

Jane: Yes.

Ted: It looked like fields or something. Is that the feeling you got?

Jane: Yes, the house was out in a field or something. I remember it was a barn type house with a wall near a cave or something. There was a man, but I couldn't see the guy. All I knew was that I had to get by him somehow to get to Justin. In the second dream, I was on a bridge like a sand bridge. There was shooting between the police and some criminals. I think I did get Justin back in that dream.

Ted: What did Justin look like? The same as when he disappeared?

Jane: Yes.

Ted: I mean he didn't look older?

Jane: No, in the second dream I'm again going out my door looking down the street. Justin is coming up the street. We both started racing toward each other and I woke up and that's it.

After the interviews and before a second meeting with Jane and Robin, Ted used his powers of suggestion in hypnotic sessions with his partner, Irma, and his fifteen-year-old daughter Kelly.

Ted used hyper-suggestibility techniques after putting Irma in a hypnotic state, where she would accept everything he said without censorship. Having digested the background information from her interviews with Jane and Robin, and responding to Ted's techniques of direct and indirect suggestion and visualization, Irma was told that she was five-year-old Justin Doherty:

Ted: Justin, I'm going to let Irma use her vocal cords, and we're going to talk to you. I don't want you to be afraid, because I am here to help you, and you are going to be able to talk through Irma. Now Irma, you are going to let Justin talk to you through you, but he has to go through your higher conscious level, which is always with you. Justin is now in your body and he is able to talk. We are going to talk about the day you didn't come home. Were you playing that day?

Justin: Yes.

Ted: Why did you leave the projects where you were playing?

Justin: The kids were fighting.

Ted: When you left the kids did you go alone?

Justin: Yes.

Ted: All right, what happened when you went home, did you go all the way home?

Justin: No.

Ted: Did you stay someplace?

Justin: Down by the gray building.

Ted: Is it near your house?

Justin: Kind of.

Ted: Is it a block or two away?

Justin: I don't know.

Ted: Is it near where you were playing?

Justin: It's next to the fire station.

Ted: What happened that prevented you from going home?

Justin: A man was behind me.

Ted: What did he look like?

Justin: Tall with a beard.
Ted: Was he with anyone else?
Justin: Yes, another man with a white shirt.
Frank: Did he have a beard too?
Justin: No.
Ted: The man who came up behind you, what did he do?
Justin: He asked me if I wanted to take a ride with him.
Ted: What did you say?
Justin: I didn't say anything.

Ted and Irma continued in this manner for a long time. The nearly twenty legal size page transcript of their dialogue focused on Justin's abduction by a bearded man who forced him into his truck with another man and drove to Saugus Pond and the St. Matthew's Cemetery area near the pond.

Ted then performed hypnotic suggestion regarding Justin's abduction on his daughter Kelly, even though she was not present for the initial interviews with Jane and Robin. Ted and Irma later returned to Suffork Street with Kelly where another hypnotic technique was employed.

Irma explains in her transcript:

"The reason for bringing Kelly to Hopeville was to 'rehypnotize' her to see if she could give us any information that might be helpful. We needed a subject who had little or no previous knowledge or information about the case. Kelly was totally unfamiliar with the area or the particulars of the case. Her mind was therefore free and open to Ted's hypnotic suggestion.

"We walked up Sussex Lane, the roadway that led to the cemetery and Saugus Pond where Ted gave Kelly hypnotic suggestion. We then asked Kelly to lead us. She led us down the roadway into the woods along a path. We climbed over a stone wall and past some large fir trees. Behind the fir trees, Kelly stopped and stared. An area in the woods had been recently dug up, no more than a day or two, and there was a shovel lying on the ground partially hidden by a bush. We asked Kelly how she felt and she said her stomach felt nauseous, and her body felt weird, symptoms she didn't have previously.

" Kelly then led us to St. Matthew's Cemetery and we stopped at area sixty. It was a private family burial plot surrounded by disheveled stonewalls and contained about forty graves of family members, most who had died in the nineteenth century. Kelly pointed to an old, weather worn white fence. She walked around the fence and stopped abruptly at the stone grave marker and told us that she felt the same sick feelings she had previously experienced at the dug out area in the woods. Buried in the gravesite were the remains of William Henry Holland, who died peacefully in 1834.

Kelly gave this account of what happened next. "Ted then hypnotized me to get more information about this bizarre situation. In my trance, I saw a balding man with small strands of brown hair around his ears standing very still. He was shirtless and wearing dark pants. I couldn't make out his face. The time of day appeared to be evening, because there were lots of shadows. The man had something under his arm that he wrapped up and cautiously placed in the back of a light green van. I saw the name 'Dodge' on the van and regular, not commercial, license plates that read MT 320. The man was alone."

Although intriguing, the work of Ted Lyons and Irma Shelton was not helpful. No connection to current Hopeville relatives or to a light green van with an MT 320 plate number could be found. The dug out area was a grave made by a young, neighborhood boy burying his pet guinea pig.

The information generated by the investigative hypnotists simply recalled old, unproven theories about who might have seized Justin such as possibly forcing him into a vehicle and taking him away from Hopeville. The Saugus Pond and St. Matthew's Cemetery episodes detailed in Irma's transcripts were leads previously forwarded by several psychics who maintained that Justin disappeared near a body of water and was buried in a shallow grave between the cemetery and the pond. There were many bodies of water in the twenty-six square miles of Hopeville, and all had been thoroughly searched, none more than Saugus Pond.

Chapter 20

As the years after Justin's disappearance passed, Rick Thurston and his detectives actively followed up on leads from California to New England. The case would remain open until it was solved.

One interesting lead took Thurston, Monroe and State Police Detective Harold Gallagher to Chesapeake, Virginia, to locate and investigate Jane's mother and sister. Interviewing the relatives of missing children is a difficult and sensitive process, especially if some family discord exists, but good investigators must look closely for leads that may point to family involvement in crimes, particularly in kidnapping cases.

Detectives had heard that indeed there was some discord in Jane's family.

According to police records, Jane was born in Atlanta and adopted by an older woman in Bolton, Tennessee, where she grew up. When the detectives contacted her birth mother in a rundown neighborhood in Chesapeake, they learned that she first married at age twelve and gave birth to Jane at age thirteen. She was a petite woman with strawberry blond hair and a gaunt, deeply wrinkled face who smoked continually while talking to the three detectives.

Jane's mother was very forthcoming. She told the detectives that she had been married four times and had several children and stepchildren, but was now divorced. She indicated that Jane was her oldest child and because she was so young and also unmarried when Jane was born, she was forced to put Jane up for adoption. She indicated that her second husband was married to one of her older daughters. She also informed the police that she was presently unemployed and collecting Social Security disability benefits.

She stated emphatically that she had never been in Hopeville and didn't plan to go there, admitting, "I didn't like George Doherty when he lived in Virginia and I don't like him now. I do, however, still maintain contact with Jane by occasionally calling or writing her."

She denied any involvement in the disappearance of Justin. When questioned about any prior arrests, she said there were none. The detectives then searched her house with negative results.

The detectives also questioned Jane's sister at her mother's home. She was employed as a hotel maid and had been married for the past year to a longshoreman who worked in Norfolk. She had two children, a five-year-old daughter born out of wedlock and a three-year-old daughter with her present husband.

She bore a facial resemblance to Jane, but despite being five years younger than her sister; she looked older and was a much bigger woman. She had bleached blond hair and wore heavy make-up. Like her mother, she spoke freely and candidly.

She admitted she had previously dated George Doherty before he married Jane and had last seen him in 1969 prior to the Doherty family moving to Massachusetts. She stated she was last in Hopeville in August 1973 with her husband, his sister, and her brother-in-law. They only stayed for a day, and then returned to Virginia. She said that she too didn't get along with George Doherty and didn't see him while they were in Hopeville. She mentioned that Jane had called her in June 1975 and briefly provided her with the circumstances surrounding Justin's disappearance before turning to lighter topics.

Further investigation revealed that Jane's relatives had not been in Hopeville in 1975 or had any involvement in Justin's disappearance.

Calls and letters to Jane and Thurston still continued to trickle in for seven long years. One day, Thurston received a typed, unsigned letter in his mailbox:

"Justin Doherty voluntarily entered a car of a man who was not a stranger to him. Justin plays near the fire station and this man frequently visits the men in the station. He is about forty, medium height, stocky build, and has gray hair and visits bars in town. The boy is dead. His body is in a wooded area, a short distance from the Connecticut state line. Persons walking in the area will find the boy's body in a discarded trash barrel. The boy was killed because the kidnapper was afraid he would reveal his identity. The boy's death resulted from strangulation."

The letter baffled Thurston. He asked the fire chief if he knew anyone who fit the man's description. "Yeah, I know about fifty guys in town that fit that description, Rick. Do you want to interview all of them?"

A typical letter received by Jane read as follows:

"My ESP tells me you are looking for a man in his fifties, heavy set, his face badly scarred, and most of the time he wears dark glasses. He comes to a Friendly's Restaurant in your area and acts very nervous and strange and keeps throwing his head back, like he is listening to someone. I think he lives in Hopeville and his first name starts with F, and his last name with A.

"I believe he also kidnapped David Louison of Brockton. This can be checked out with some of the waiters and waitresses that waited on him last June. You will never forget his face.

"The picture of your son will go up in my shrine that will be built this summer in my yard and my first prayers will be said for his safe return. Sincerely, a Friend"

There was no Friendly's Restaurant within twenty miles of Hopeville; however, there was one in Springfield. Thurston contacted personnel there and they mentioned they see some strange people from time to time but no one that fit Thurston's sketchy description.

After tracking down hundreds of leads and giving polygraphs to over one hundred people, Jane and Rick had no better idea of what happened to Justin than they'd had at the start of the investigation. The hope of ever finding him was rapidly fading. Would Justin just be another statistic—a little boy whose name and description was tucked away with those of countless other missing children in some dusty office file cabinet? After seven years, it seemed more and more likely.

Most women in Jane's situation would be in deep depression and despair. They would be angry at God and be emotionally broken, but not Jane Doherty. She hid her intense pain and rallied her husband, dear friends, and her younger children when their spirits and hope were down and their suffering turned into sorrowful tears. Her Justin would not just be another missing child statistic! Dead or alive, he would always be in her loving heart and mind.

Chapter 21

Two women sat in Hopeville Diner after their morning shift as crossing guards at the street corner across from Meadowbrook Elementary School. Black clouds hung heavy in the sky and thunder rumbled in the distance.

"Well, I don't look forward to standing at my post at lunch time ushering the little ones home for lunch with lighting flashing at my heels. When I took this job last month I didn't think about that part it," said one woman.

Looking and smiling at her close friend, Jane Doherty said, "Come on, the school provides peanut butter and jelly sandwiches, milk, and snacks for the children if it gets too bad. The office notifies mothers and tells them their kids won't be home for lunch. Sometimes it's a tough call. But part of the job, my dear girl, is getting used to the weather. You can't let little things like that get you now."

Her friend Sandy said, "Jane Doherty, you are really something. Damm, I can't get over you. How you cope with everything amazes me. If my son were missing, I would be one big basket case and not want to talk to anybody."

"I have to talk about it, Sandy. It's my therapy. I'd go crazy if I didn't. And Justin is still alive. I know it. I can feel it. I dream about finding him all the time."

"Can you sleep at night?"

"Not really. It is near impossible to get a full night's sleep. When I lay down I think about my baby boy and pray that he's safe. The room is still and George is usually asleep. I close my eyes and picture Justin's smile and his blond hair blowing in a gentle wind. There's a warm yellow light around him. He's twelve now and tall for his age and skinny like his dad. I try to hold him tightly as long as I can, but my mind always races on to something else.

"And sometimes I dream about him being with another family.

He's safe but he isn't happy. He knows things aren't right. He misses his real family and is waiting for the right time to run away and find us."

Jane paused for a moment, and said to Sandy, "But there're nightmares too."

Conscious of other diner patrons sitting in the next booth, Sandy lowered her voice, "Can you talk about them? It might help."

"I don't know if I can. It's hard, very hard."

After several moments of silence, Jane moved closer to her friend and whispered, "I do have one horrible dream from time to time. I see a sad, gray-haired woman who's haunted by not knowing whether her son is dead or alive. She is alone, standing by an empty grave, looking up into a dark and dreary sky. The woman has no closure, no peace-- it's awful, just awful. She eventually dies a painful death without ever knowing. When I wake up, I am shaking and it takes a minute to realize that it was a dream. Then I can't get back to sleep. I lay there with a sick feeling in my stomach and crying quietly so as not to disturb George.

"I haven't talked about this with other people, not even George. Now only you know and please, please keep this to yourself. I had to tell someone. I have to be strong for my family, but my heart is broken. I don't want my family to worry about me. Do you understand?

"Yes, Jane, I do."

"I know I'm a good mother, Sandy. I watch my children very closely and love them dearly. I protect my children. For God sakes, Justin was playing with his brother in the neighborhood just like he always did. I replay that Sunday in my mind over and over again. Should I have protected him more? I struggle with those thoughts. I'm just beginning to accept the fact that some things happen that are out of our control. There are no answers."

"Why do you think God allowed this awful thing happen to you and your family?" Sandy asked.

"I don't know. I ask myself that question all the time. I don't go to church; I've never been very religious. For a while, I wondered if God was punishing me for not being faithful."

Seeing the pain and suffering on her friend's face for the first time, Sandy said, "Some people who face tragedy say they only get through it because of their faith. That God has a reason and loves them in spite of life's cruelties."

"I've heard that. Down deep I feel I have faith in God. But for a long time I was really angry with Him. Why did He do this to my family? Why didn't He keep Justin safe? I kept asking those questions.

"But I'm not angry with Him anymore. I haven't had an easy life, but I have a loving family and two other children I adore. One of my children has been taken from me and I have asked God why? I don't have the answer. Someday He may give me the answer. I now pray to Him to keep me strong and help me find my child. I also need to be there for my family and conserve the little energy I have to find my baby and bring him home. I can't afford to be angry."

"Jane, I must tell you how much I admire you. Someday, God will give you answers. You must have faith and trust in him."

Jane reached for Sandy's hand and gave it a gentle squeeze as tears filled both women's eyes.

Chapter 22

In 1982, Norman Stedman was twenty-three, unemployed, and living with his father. His dad worked as a local school custodian and reserve policeman and ate many of his meals out. He was rarely at home leaving Norman alone in his house or sitting on the curbside in front of his Suffork Street house.

Norman finally had all the privacy he needed. He could invite teenage neighborhood boys into his house for drinking parties without anyone stopping him or asking embarrassing questions. His bedroom was now his inner sanctum, off limits to his father, inhabited only by Norman and his black, mangy cat, a poor creature he loved to torment. His stepmother and grandmother were dead now and Norman was free from their constant nagging and endless scrutiny.

Norman welcomed his new freedom. He had an opportunity to feed his suppressed sexual appetite and ease the rage that was steadily simmering inside him, ready to explode at any moment. Now reading extensively, he was seen often, lumbering to the town library carrying a lumpy book bag.

Unfortunately, his new freedom did not bring him happiness since his loneliness and rejection by his past high school and college classmates and teachers still ate away at him. Even the young boys in the neighborhood avoided him, thinking he was some type of freak. He started to drink heavily. Beer and vodka were his favorites. When he was alone and got drunk, he could escape from his hopeless world to a surreal place where he was loved and adored by dead people. Mystical and creative fantasies rushed through his head. The memories of some of his stupors served as material for the poems and essays he busily wrote in the quiet of his bedroom.

There was however one exception. It was one thing that gave him identity and acceptance. It was local theatre. It was the only place where he could escape his diabolic feelings. He could be someone else there. He was grateful that the North County Community Players appreciated the work he did for their organization. It gave him quiet satisfaction and true enjoyment.

A theatre group thrives on having diverse personalities and since the Community Players needed as much volunteer help as they could get, it was easy for him to fit in comfortably.

Norman was always in the library auditorium where the Players gathered, helping with all aspects of their theatrical productions. He was hard working and reliable, the type who learned his lines cold, without a slip-up. He was especially excited about the role he had recently played in Agatha Christie's *Mousetrap*—the character of a murder suspect. He chuckled to himself thinking it was perfect casting.

Norman once worked part-time in Hopeville Hospital as an operating room orderly, where one of his major duties was cleaning the surgical instruments after operations. He liked his job and did it well. His fascination with blood, death, and the afterlife took on new dimensions during this time. Always a voracious reader, he buried himself in macabre books and with his offbeat writing that focused on death and dying.

Although his hospital work was satisfactory, he was reprimanded twice by hospital officials for poor personal hygiene and sent home to change his clothes. This enraged him.

"Who the hell are they to tell me I can't be myself? There is no dress code!" he yelled at his father, who tried to convince him to heed the hospital's warnings.

"Screw them, their idiots. I'm quitting."

Norman knew his physical appearance made people uneasy. He was six-foot, 250 plus pounds, with curly, oily black hair and slovenly muttonchops. He wore black horned-rim glasses that slipped off his bulbous nose, and black baggy shirts and pants that were rarely changed or washed. He blinked constantly, talked with a lisp, and at times reeked body odor. He acted as though it didn't bother him if people thought that he was strange, even repulsive, but he refused to do anything about his appearance and distracting body odor.

He compensated by deliberately cultivating an ominous demeanor, like one of the villains he played, and did play with some success, in his theatre's performances. One of his favorite roles was that of King

Herod in *Jesus Christ Super Star,* for which he received positive reviews from some of his fellow actors.

However, in real life he experienced rejection constantly from other neighborhood children he tried to befriend as a child, from heckling high school classmates who called him "Tuba" and "Earthquake," and from bullying "jocks" who teased him in the school corridors.

Even in the theater, maybe the only place he had ever felt somewhat accepted, they began to reject him. When he enrolled in theatre and creative writing classes at the local college, he auditioned for every play. However, the auditions were more competitive than any in high school or with the North Community Players. He got one small role in *Charley's Aunt* early on, but in the nearly three years that followed, nothing. He couldn't understand why he was being blackballed.

Always persisting, he auditioned for musical productions on six different occasions, each time singing the same song. The song lyrics appealed to Norman since it described a person who was lonely, but didn't want to be an insecure person and didn't want to live all by himself without love. It was Norman's theme song, a cry for help from a desperate, disturbed man.

He was rejected in all of his auditions. Later, he discovered that some of his theatre classmates had a habit of mocking him. They would gather around a piano and mimic him singing, accentuating his lisp and mannerisms to uproarious laughter. When he inadvertently heard his classmates mocking him, it greatly depressed him. It was the same sick feeling he experienced back in high school when once during a rehearsal, other student actors snickered back stage when the leading lady refused to give him a kiss on the cheek.

As much as all his rejections hurt, Norman never shared his feelings with other people. There was no one he trusted enough to confide in. He was like a recluse on a deserted island, with only his fantasy life to keep him sane. Although he had become adept at masking his inner torment with his grotesque exterior and muted personality, his rage was escalating to a point where it could no longer be controlled, even beyond the point it had been prior to his murdering Justin. Maybe a part of him wanted to be caught and put away. It would give him the notoriety he craved, but at the same time he was afraid of what might happen to him. He didn't want to be put in prison for life as a child killer and although he thought about it frequently, suicide wasn't an option either.

He now felt he had to do something bold to ease his uncontrollable pain and fury or else he would go totally insane and unable to function. Bizarre thoughts flooded his mind. He had to exercise power over someone. One thing was for sure. He had fooled people before, and he could do it again.

Chapter 23

Before the Dohertys moved to Center Street, Bud and Gloria Richmond had lived three houses down from them on Suffork Street. The Richmonds were true "Townies" born and raised in Hopeville. They had two children, a sixteen-year-old daughter Sally, and a fourteen-year-old son, Donnie.

Bud and George Doherty became fast friends through a common interest in repairing, refinishing, and painting what they called, "old jalopies." George was the master mechanic and Bud the skilled auto body man. Many nights, the garage lights were blazed brightly in one of their garages as both men tinkered in the greasy bowels of an old vehicle, somehow resuscitating it to be sold to a waiting buyer weeks later with a nifty profit. Bud eventually opened his own body shop outside the town limits and established a reputation as an honest, hard-working man in a tough, competitive business.

Bud was a personable, tall and strong looking fellow with rosy cheeks and a thick crop of reddish-brown hair. But in spite of his friendly appearance, he was, as locals said,

"The type of man whose dander you wouldn't want to stir up."

On the other hand, he was a caring and sensitive man who reached out and tried to comfort George and Jane during the period when Justin was missing. He later became a born-again Christian, and was one of the few people who Jane sought out for spiritual advice throughout her long ordeal.

Gloria Richmond was what they called in Hopeville, "a piece of work." A cute brunette with an engaging smile, she possessed a keen sense of humor, boundless energy, and strong opinions that she didn't hesitate to share. Like her husband, she was someone you'd want as a friend, but definitely wouldn't want as an enemy. She was also a descendent of George Suffork, who had built most of the houses on the street named after him and lived with her family in the old homestead at the end of Suffork.

Not only were Bud and George close friends, but in 1982 their two fourteen-year-old sons were inseparable, playing baseball, football and every conceivable game together with other neighborhood kids, as well as lifting weights and working out on the punching bag in Bud's garage. Bud's father had been a professional boxer and taught him the nuances of self-defense. Bud, in turn, took the two skinny young boys under his wing and spent considerable time, as he put it, "Toughening up the two kids so no one would take advantage of them."

Because of the weightlifting and boxing routine his father put him through, Donnie Richmond had developed into a wiry, 116-pound fourteen-year-old boy of average height with surprising upper body strength. He also was the local paperboy known for his reliability and good nature.

Bud and Gloria were convinced that Justin had been forcibly grabbed and thrown into a vehicle that sped out of town on that fateful day in May 1975. They prayed that he was still alive somewhere, but as the years passed without a single clue to his disappearance, they privately believed he had become one of the thousands of other missing boys in the country who are never found.

Bud and Gloria were certain that Justin wouldn't go off voluntarily with anyone, stranger or otherwise. Gloria remembered him as a "very, quiet and shy boy who wouldn't even respond to you when you spoke to him." Bud further elaborated, "I was close to the family and in his house often and still he would back off from me and retreat to his mother when I tried to talk to him. He stuck to her like Velcro."

In April 1982, an incident occurred that changed Bud and Gloria's lives forever. They would soon learn that their children were vulnerable to fatal harm from a sexual predator that lived nearby. The killer of Justin Doherty was about to attack another young boy.

It was a bleak, rainy day as light rain mist filled the sky. Bud Richmond arrived home weary from a grueling day at his auto body shop, a little after 6 p.m. When he entered his kitchen, he noticed a handwritten note from his wife informing him she had gone to pick up their daughter at the dentist.

He yelled several times for his son Donnie, and after getting no response went upstairs to his son's bedroom. Donnie wasn't there.

He checked the garage for Donnie's bike, and saw it was still there. "Where's he? He hasn't delivered papers yet?" Bud wondered. "He must be with Joey Doherty. If not, Joey will know where he is."

Bud called Joey who said the last time he saw Donnie was about 2:30 p.m. But he didn't know his whereabouts after that. "That's strange," thought Bud, "His closest buddy not knowing where he is.?"

Bud called his brother-in-law and some of his friends who lived in the surrounding streets. He also called several of his close neighbors asking them to ask their kids if they had seen Donnie. After his calls, he rushed out his door and walked up and down Suffork Street asking kids and anyone else he saw, "Have you seen Donnie?" No one had.

Usually, by the time Bud returned from work, Donnie had already been home and left again to pick up his newspapers and start his delivery route. Bud noticed that surprisingly his son's newspapers were still in a pile at the foot of his driveway. As his brow started to sweat, he suddenly thought, "trumpet lessons!" He scaled the front stairs, ran into Donnie's bedroom, and opened the closet to see if he had taken his trumpet. A question suddenly occurred to him, "Was it Thursday when he took his lesson?" Then he saw the trumpet case nestled in the corner of the closet.

"Where is he? Where's my kid?" he shouted. Bud could feel it in his bones that something was terribly wrong. Now feeling a tinge of panic, he quickly grabbed the phone, called George Doherty and asked him to help him find Donnie.

George rushed to Bud's house sensing the fear in his friend's voice. When he climbed into George's car, a worried Bud said, "You know Donnie is a very conscientious young kid. He never would just disappear and not leave a note. He always delivered his papers on time. His bike is still in the garage. My God, George, don't tell me some horrible thing has happened to my son!"

George looked down and said nothing. They drove around the neighborhood and headed for the Saugus Pond area where Donnie went fishing but still, no sign of him.

George drove a visibly distraught Bud back to his house and dropped him off. Walking across his front lawn, Bud spotted Donnie with next-door neighbor, Norman Stedman, standing on the front porch. He screamed, "Where the hell have you been?"

"Dad, I'm sorry, so sorry." Donnie was shaking and crying, looking very distraught.

"What's wrong, son?" Bud asked.

Norman spoke up. With his pronounced lisp and twitching nervously said, "Donnie was at my house drinking booze and got sick. You can call the police if you want."

"What'd you mean?" Bud screamed. "You get my son drunk and then you tell me to call the police, if I want. You idiot!"

Now out of control, Bud punched Norman repeatedly in the head and stomach, with his quick, powerful hands. In one vigorous motion, he grabbed Norman and tossed his 250-pound portly body to the ground, flailing. Neighbors rushed out of their houses to witness the ruckus. They heard Bud's booming voice, "You get up the road and if I ever see you around my son again, I'll give you another beating."

Norman got up and gathering himself in spite of his pain and dizziness said softly,

"O.K. I won't bother your son again."

Feeling the onset of a massive, throbbing headache, Norman walked in his crab-like shuffle back to his house, wondering how he would ever get out of the awful mess he'd just created.

Chapter 24

Soon after Norman left, Gloria Richmond returned home with her daughter and saw how shaken her son was. When she hugged him and tried to console him, she noticed a bright red circle around his entire neck. It looked like a severe bruise.

"Donnie what is that ugly red mark around your neck?"

"It's where Norman tried to choke me with a scarf," he muttered, still teary eyed.

"I was lucky to wake up in time and get my hand between the scarf and my neck so he didn't cut off my windpipe. I begged him to stop. Mom, I really did! He just wouldn't stop."

"What? Bud, did you know that this kid was being strangled? God, he could have died!" With her body shaking and her temper rising, Gloria yelled, "What the hell is going on here!"

"Yeah, said Bud. " I knew there was something not right about that weirdo! We need to call the police now and then get Donnie to the emergency room right away."

Patrolman Hal McVey received their complaint call and immediately drove to the Richmond house where Bud repeated all that Donnie had told him. He mentioned that when he ran up and down the street looking for Donnie, he passed Norman but didn't directly question him because the kids standing next to him said they hadn't seen Donnie. Norman had said nothing. McVey later surmised that at that time Donnie must have been passed out in Norman's bedroom while Bud was searching the streets and the pond area with George.

After hearing Bud's story, a light bulb suddenly went on in McVey's head. Looking intently at Bud he said, "I have known Norman for many years and don't trust him. I think he might have had something to do with the Justin Doherty case."

Bud quickly responded, "Damm right! After what happened with my son, I agree. That guy is really sick."

As he drove out of Bud's driveway, McVey was stopped by Norman's father, who pulled up in his truck. Fred Stedman was livid. He said that Bud had assaulted his son and he wanted Norman to file an assault charge.

"Donnie wanted to see what it felt like to get drunk and I tried to stop him, but he wouldn't listen," was the excuse Norman had given his father.

McVey wasted no words, "Listen Fred, your son is in serious trouble. He may be booked for attempted murder. I want you and Norman to come down to the station to give statements as soon as possible. The Richmonds will give their statements later tonight after they go to the hospital."

Fred Stedman's angry tone quickly changed, "Oh," he softly sputtered. "We'll be down after supper."

Hal McVey had been a Hopeville police officer for four years and loved the law enforcement business. He was perceptive, courteous and a quick study to boot.

As he drove back to the police station his mind fixed on images of Norman. He thought about that late Sunday afternoon about seven years ago when Justin disappeared. He was a police intern at the time and was visiting his fiancée, whose house was on a street parallel to Suffork and backed up to the Stedman's property. He remembered the Suffork neighbors scurrying around their backyards calling Justin's name. He had watched Norman and his father search their own yard, and neighboring yards as well. He thought about the bizarre stories his fiancée had told him about playing with Norman when she was a young teenager, describing sexual advances he made on her girl friends. Norman had definitely had some problems when growing up, now as an adult he seemed to be even more disturbed.

Hal started to do some math. When Justin disappeared, Norman would have been sixteen and just a junior in high school, pretty young to commit a crime like kidnapping a young boy. Still it could be possible, very possible.

Hal remembered that people had mocked Norman, ignored him, or gone out of their way to be nice to him. He chose the latter approach. He sensed that Norman didn't want to be pitied, so he avoided any suggestion of pity. When he spoke to Norman he was respectful and upbeat; he tried to make him feel like a worthwhile human being.

Norman didn't appear to resent his easy, pleasant manner. McVey believed that Norman respected him as a person and as a police officer. But then, it was difficult to get a good read on what Norman really thought about anybody or anything.

In fact, Hal McVey did have pity for Norman. He suspected that Norman suffered from a major personality disorder. But could he be a sociopath killer? The more he pondered the question, the clearer it became to him that the answer was "yes." There was no doubt now, that Norman was capable of violence; how had he been so blind to that possibility until now? How had everybody? The guy is sick and needs help. All these years no one had thought to question Norman Stedman about the disappearance of Justin Doherty. My God, thought McVey, lead us to the truth!

In the next few hours, McVey and others would interrogate Norman for what apparently was an attempted murder of Donnie. He for one didn't trust Norman to tell the truth or provide all the necessary details, but he knew that because of his amicable relationship with Norman he would play a crucial role in getting him to confess to any crime he might have committed. He also knew that the interrogation wouldn't stop with questions strictly about the Donnie Richmond incident.

Chapter 25

Accompanied by his parents, Donnie arrived at the police station to give his statement.

Q. During the afternoon hours today, Thursday, April 15, 1982, did you go to someone's house?
A. Yes, I went to Norman Stedman's house.

Q. What is Norman's address? And also describe the house.
A. It is a green house with white trim with one of the front windows broken. It is on Suffork Street, the same street as mine.

Q. What time did you go there?
A. About 3 p.m.

Juvenile Detective Jeff Childs took Donnie Richmond's statement while McVey assisted and served as a witness. Childs was a burly fellow in his early thirties with a ruddy complexion, a smart crew cut and little rolls beginning to form around the mid-section of his six foot two frame. He did double duty as a detective and police photographer and had taken a photo of Donnie's neck while Bud Richmond gave his witness statement to McVey.

The Richmonds had visited the Hopeville Hospital earlier in the evening to have Donnie's neck examined and treated. The emergency doctor on duty had initially thought he was treating a large rope burn, saying it was similar to what you would see on a lynching victim. Gloria Richmond didn't appreciate the comment.

Donnie's admission that he went to Norman's house around 3 p.m. and Bud's statement that he arrived home from work at 6:15 p.m. meant that Donnie had spent over three hours in Norman's house.

Q. Donnie, when you went to Norman's house, in your own words, what happened?"

A. Norman was sitting on the sidewalk curb where he usually does and asked me to go inside his house and have something to drink. I said all right, just to shut him up, because he had asked me several times in the past to stop in for a drink. We then went to his house and he asked me to go upstairs to his bedroom because someone might see us. I had a few beers and then he convinced me to have some Vodka. After he took a sip, I finished what was left in the bottle. I then had one more beer and started to feel bad. The room was spinning and I almost fell asleep at that time. He realized that I wasn't feeling good so he tried to massage me to make me feel better."

Q. Where did he massage you?
A. On the shoulders.

Q. He didn't massage your neck?
A. No, just my shoulders.

Q. What happened next?
A. He finally got me up and I wasn't feeling good at all and everything was still spinning. He convinced me to go downstairs and have a cup of coffee, because he knew he was in trouble. I had a coffee and finally fell on the kitchen floor because I was in such bad shape. I was shivering and almost asleep when he got me a pillow. And then I went to sleep.

Q. How long did you sleep?
A. Hard to tell. It must have been awhile.

Q. What happened when you finally woke up?
A. I started to vomit about three or four times and I was crying because it hurt. I then went back to sleep and when I woke up this time Norman was strangling me with a rag around my neck.

Q. Can you describe the rag?
A. It was brownish and looked like a handkerchief.

Q. How was the rag around your neck?
A. The rag was all around my neck. Norman was sitting on my back and I couldn't breathe. The rag was so tight that I realized that he was choking off my wind. I felt he was trying to kill me. I managed to get the rag loosened by putting my fingers under it.

Q. You think he was trying to kill you?
A. I think he was because my hand was turning real red.

Q. What happened next?
A. When I got the rag off, I said we should go down to my house and explain what had happened. He kept saying to me to get sobered up. I wanted to see my father and explain what had happened because I knew he would be worried.

Q. At any time did you hear Norman say that he was going to kill you?
A. No, I did not hear that, but I kept saying to him that he was trying to kill me when he had the rag around my neck and told him to stop. But he wouldn't stop.

Q. How were you able to talk?
A. It was when I got my fingers under the rag when I told him he was killing me. He said he wasn't trying to but he was trying to sober me up.

Q. What was his reply when you said to come down to the house and talk to your father?
A. He told me to tell my father that I was somewhere else.

Q. Does Norman live with anyone?
A. He lives with his father, Fred Stedman.

Q. Do you know Norman very well?
A. Yes, I have known him since I have been delivering papers to his house, about two years now.

Q. Can you describe what Norman looks like?
A. He has a mustache, a few hairs on his chin; he is fat, very slow walking.

Q. How tall is he?
A. About six feet.

Q. How old is he?
A. About twenty-three or twenty-four.

Q. What was he wearing today?
A. Blue slacks, a checkered shirt, and dress type shoes.

Q. If you saw him again could you recognize him?
A. Yes.

Q. Is there anything else you would like to add to this statement?
A. Only that every time I have seen him he has told me to come up for a drink.

Q. Did he make any sexual advances toward you?
A. Only when he tried to massage my shoulders. Nothing other than that can I remember.

Q. Has Norman ever had you in his house before to drink? And has he ever bought you alcohol before?
A. No and no he has not.

Q. Do you know of other kids he had over to drink that were underage?
A. Yes, some have gotten drunk too.

Q. Do you want to press charges?
A. Yes.

Q. Is everything you have said the truth?
A. Yes, it is the truth.

As Donnie and his parents left the conference room, Childs received a call from the first floor receptionist informing him that Norman and Fred Stedman were waiting downstairs. "Tell them I will be down to get them in a few minutes," he said as he looked intently at the blank expression on McVey's face. They were both thinking the same thing.

Chapter 26

A jittery Norman Stedman, with his father at his side, entered the conference room to give his statement. Childs and McVey knew that their questions had to focus on the current charges of attempted murder and contributing to the delinquency of a minor. Their suspicions of Norman's involvement in the Justin Doherty case would have to wait.

Earlier that evening, McVey felt compelled to write a memo to Rick Thurston and the new chief of police, Paul Velone:

"I have known Norman Stedman for approximately twelve years, having at one time lived in the Suffork Street area. My wife knew him even longer and told me that he had a habit of pinching girls' breasts while playing basketball in junior high school. I knew Norman to be a loner and very strange. He might also be homosexual. My brother-in-law and several other males who lived a street or two over from Suffork knew Norman and are almost certain that Norman made obscene calls to them, because they recognized his voice and he used to stare at them while they were working out at the YMCA."

Chief Velone had replaced Chief Sawyer six months earlier. He agreed with Thurston that it was advisable to have Childs and McVey first concentrate on questioning Norman about the Donnie Richmond complaint, and then bring him back the next morning for questions relating specifically to the Justin Doherty case.

Velone was almost the complete opposite of his predecessor, Chief Sawyer. A Boston native, he had recently retired as a state police detective after having gained considerable notoriety for investigating and prosecuting several high profile Mafia figures. He was in his early forties, a good-looking, highly professional, urbane "spit and polish" type of guy—one of a new breed of chiefs that were being hired in smaller communities around the state.

Velone took pride in his investigative skills, given the number of extensive investigations he had conducted while with the state police.

After reading McVey's memo, he decided to take full control of the Doherty investigation and relegated Thurston to a secondary role. He immediately arranged a meeting with Childs and McVey to advise them before their interrogation of Norman.

With McVey and Fred Stedman present as witnesses, Childs read Norman a copy of his constitutional rights, gave the copy to him, and began his questions:

Q. On the afternoon of April 15, 1982, did you talk to Donnie Richmond while you were on Suffork Street?
A. Yes.

Q. What time did you talk to him?
A. About 3:30 or 3:45 p.m.

Q. Did you ask him to come into your house, or your father's house where you live?
A. Yes, I did.

Q. Once inside your house, did you take Donnie to your bedroom?
A. He asked me if he could have a beer and that's when I said yes.

Q. What kind?
A. I'm not sure.

Q. Did you then go to your bedroom, after you gave him the beer?
A. We were in the bedroom at the time and I had beer in my bedroom.

Q. How much beer did you give him?
A. Two cans.

Q. Did you give him anything else to drink?
A. A little vodka. He asked me if he could try it and I said yes. He took the bottle and took a swallow and then I took one swallow. I put it back on the shelf and that's when he took it and finished it.

Q. What did you do then?
A. He asked me if I would give him a massage, so I did.

Q. Did anything else happen?

A. No.

Q. Where did you both go then?
A. Downstairs to the kitchen. I fixed him a cup of coffee and he had a little and just flopped down on the kitchen floor. I called his father at work a couple of times, but the line was busy. When I saw his father's truck go down the street, I shook him trying to wake him and get him home. After a little bit he awoke and drank a little cold water and went outside and sat in the fresh air. I took him down to his house, but at the time we arrived his parents weren't there. His father then pulled into the driveway. I told his father he could call the police if he wanted to but that we had been to my house and had a couple of drinks. At which point, Donnie's father attacked me and punched me a few times and threw me down. I then went up to my house and called my father and asked him if he could come home.

Q. While you were in the kitchen, did you take a cloth and place it around Donnie's neck?
A. That's how I shook him awake. I thought the shock would wake him up. It was the only thing I could think of to do to get him awake enough to get him to go down the street. He had been sleeping quite awhile.

Q. Did he at any time tell you to stop choking him?
A. Yes he did, and I did. It probably came out a little harder than I wanted it to, but I wanted to wake him up.

Q. Where is the rag you used?
A. Still in the kitchen. It was not a rag. It was a red, white, and yellow scarf. I figured that a shock to his system would be the only way to wake him up.

Q. What do you mean when you say a shock to his system?
A. I couldn't think of any way to wake him up. I tried to throw cold water on him, shaking him and poking him.

Q. Did you think choking him would wake him up?
A. That's why I did it. I didn't try to choke him hard.

Q. What time was this when you were trying to wake him up by shaking and choking him?
A. I think it was around 5 or 5:30 p.m.

Q. Why didn't you just take him home by carrying him rather than choking him?
A. I could not lift him off the floor; he was dead weight.

Q. Why didn't you just go down and get his parents to come get him?
A. That didn't occur to me.

Q. But choking him to wake him up did?
A. The only thing I could think of was shock. I tried ice. I couldn't think of anything else to do to wake him up. I put it around his neck once and pulled hard.

Q. How much do you weigh?"
A. Over 250 pounds.

Q. How tall are you?
A. Six foot.

Q. How much do you think Donnie weighs?
A. About 160 pounds (note: Donnie's actual weight was 116 lbs)

Q. Were you scared that you might get in trouble if he couldn't wake up?
A. Yes, but I was scared more about him.

Q. Has something like this happened to you before?
A. No.

Q. Why then did you get so worried?
A. I was scared for him and for me.

Q. Have you ever been drunk yourself before?
A. Yes.

Q. Have you ever passed out?
A. No.

Q. Have you ever seen other people pass out before?
A. No, but I have seen people drunk before.

Q. Have you ever had anyone else over to your house before who is a minor to drink alcohol?
A. Yes, about a year ago.

Childs started probing to see if Norman had made sexual advances during the time Donnie was drunk or asleep. Norman only admitted to massaging Donnie's "back and front." He denied engaging in any sexual activity with him. He did imply that Donnie wanted him to participate in some sexual acts, but Norman said that he did not agree to do what Donnie wanted.

After further investigation, the police concluded that Norman was deliberately lying, attempting to shift blame to Donnie to create an embarrassing situation for the Richmonds and cause them to drop the charges.

The police felt Donnie was "a solid and honest boy." They believed his story about waking up just in time, before Norman could have done unspeakable things to him. In the final analysis, the police found no evidence of sexual assault and no such charges were brought against Norman.

Although he panicked when Donnie suddenly freed himself, Norman was shrewd in his hurried concoction of a scenario he thought the police might accept, one in which his intentions were grossly misinterpreted. He may have been wrong in getting a minor drunk, but he wouldn't strangle him. He was trying to sober him up by shocking him.

Donnie was the one that coaxed him into giving him a drink, Donnie was the one that finished the whole bottle of vodka and Donnie was the one who wanted sex.

Although Norman may have acted spontaneously in luring Donnie into his bedroom, his plan to get Donnie inside the house appears premeditated. From his daily haunt on the front curbside, he closely observed neighborhood children and their parents. He knew their habits and their work schedules. He knew he would have at least three hours alone with Donnie. He had been pestering Donnie to join him in a drink for a long time, usually when Donnie was delivering newspapers.

This time Norman asked Donnie not to bring his bike with him, since it would alert people to his whereabouts.

Fred Stedman later confirmed that Norman had an occasional drinking party in the house with a couple of men his age, but it must have been only when he was alone there that he asked underage boys to drink with him. When Norman gave his statement to police, he claimed only one other teenager before Donnie had ever visited his bedroom for a drink. Police later determined this to be an outright lie. Norman had invited several young boys into his house for a drink and more than one boy had accepted. Fortunately, none of the others had passed out and been at his mercy.

In his testimony Norman exaggerated Donnie's weight (160 pounds of dead weight versus Donnie's actual weight of 116 pounds) when he tried to explain why he didn't consider more reasonable methods of waking Donnie up other than choking him. He obviously thought skinny Donnie was weak and would be easy to strangle to death, but he had miscalculated the boy's strength.

Norman had also miscalculated his ability to deceive Childs and McVey. They saw enough inconsistencies in his testimony to give them sufficient cause to charge him with contributing to the delinquency of a minor and with assault with intent to commit murder. They handcuffed him and put him in the holding cell on the first floor of the police station. They clearly had more to talk to him about in the morning.

After the interrogation, McVey got Fred Stedman to sign a "Consent to Search" form and went to the house to find the red, white, and yellow scarf. When he returned to the police station with it, Norman identified it as the item he had used to choke Donnie.

Chapter 27

The Hopeville Police Station was a new state of the art facility. It was a handsome two story building of imitation gray brick with forest green trim, situated on newly landscaped grounds and surrounded on the periphery by large, stately oak trees.

The new building was a source of pride to the community and to the police and rescue personnel who worked there. A modern interrogation room, spacious conference rooms, and attractively furnished offices for the chief and detectives were on the second floor.

The main lobby reception area and dispatcher, technology and communications offices were on the first floor, along with several other small rooms for officers to use.

In the basement were cells for prisoners and those temporary visitors who stayed in the "holding area" overnight to sober up.

The cells were surprisingly pleasant looking and were painted in light pastels, a change from the dingy gray found in most cells. An exposed bathroom was accessible in each unit with a twin bed on one side of the room. There was a small gray rectangular steel table and two sturdy oak chairs bolted to the floor. The cells looked like tiny, one-room efficiency apartments except for the bolted furniture and two blinking security cameras conspicuously located high on the sidewalls. Of course, the locked steel door at the cell entrance clearly indicated that this wasn't an efficiency apartment somewhere in suburbia.

Later that evening, Detective Childs went to Norman's cell and asked him if he could talk to him for a few minutes.

A wary Norman said, "Sure."

After again reading him his rights, Childs began a discussion that he had rehearsed in his mind for the past few hours. "Knowing what we heard today about your actions with the Richmond boy, we think you might know something about what happened to Justin Doherty. You must know the anguish the Doherty family has endured for such a long time. If you have done something really wrong, here is your opportunity to get penance from the Lord. I suggest you talk to either your priest or a minister and think about this."

Norman showed no facial reaction. He said nothing, although his body did begin to shake slightly.

As he turned to walk away, Childs said, "I don't want to talk to you any more tonight. I want you to really think about all this overnight. I'll be talking to you in the morning."

The next morning, Norman was brought upstairs to the interrogation room. Detective Harrison was present with Childs and McVey, but left quickly because he felt the two policemen had already established rapport with Norman and were the best ones to continue with the questioning. He was also concerned that three officers in the room were too many and might be subject to future criticism and claims from the Norman's lawyers of intimidating and squeezing false testimony out of him.

Harrison stared at Norman before he left the interrogation room. Looking him squarely in his beady eyes, he sensed something he had seen before in a number of criminal interrogations over the years, "You look at them and they look at you and you know they are going to give it up."

The previous evening, Fred Stedman and his minister, Pastor John Hobson of the Hopeville Baptist Church had visited Norman at the police station. Because of the opportunity to sing with a church group and gain acceptance with other high school musicians, Norman had attended St. Matthew's Catholic Church. In actual fact, he had little use for formal religion.

Although he had no idea of Norman's religious orientation, Childs was hoping that Norman would at least listen to his father's pastor. He said to McVey, "Maybe the two men made some headway with Norman last night after I left and he's ready to come clean. My advice to Norman to confide to a member of the clergy might not have been as farfetched as I initially thought. Hopefully, I'm right for a change."

The next morning, Childs again read Norman his rights and then began his questioning. McVey was surprised to see a highly agitated Norman suddenly become tight-lipped and refuse to say anything to Childs.

"Norman, you have known me for years," McVey said in a soothing voice. "You need to answer Detective Childs' questions. Whatever you say, we are here to protect you. That's our job. I know there is something heavy on your chest. It's all right to tell us and you need to tell us now."

Shaking violently, Norman started to cry. His large body slumped over the conference table; heavy tears fogged his glasses and streamed down his mustache and hairy cheeks. He was now hyperventilating.

"Norman listen. I want to again reassure you that we'll protect you no matter what," McVey said.

Eventually, Norman calmed down, nodded his head, and agreed to answer Childs' questions.

Chapter 28

Childs resumed his questioning as he looked across the table at a weary looking and highly nervous Norman. McVey continued to sit in as a witness.

Q. Did you know Justin Doherty?
A. Not personally, just as a kid on the street.

Q. Do you remember when he disappeared?
A. Yes, it was 1975 because I was sixteen.

Q. What grade were you in at the time in school?
A. A junior. I was in theatre class and the next day we went on a field trip to Stratford, Connecticut to see *Hamlet*.

Q. Did you have anything to do with the disappearance of Justin Doherty?
A. Yes.

Q. In your own words tell me what happened.
A. It was a Sunday. I was alone at home that day and I saw Justin walking up the street. I had always thought it would be easy to kill someone and easy to get away with it, some form of fun.

Q. Did you invite Justin into your house?
A. Yes, I did.

Q. After he came into your house, what happened?
A. We went into the kitchen. The shades were down. I grabbed his mouth from behind. I took a knife and swung it into his chest.

Q. What kind of knife did you use?
A. I think it was a kitchen knife, but I'm not really sure.

Q. Do you remember what Justin was wearing that day?
A. No, I don't.

Q. Do you remember about how old he was?
A. Five or six.

Q. After you stabbed him, what did you do with the body?
A. I put it in a plastic trash bag and temporarily placed it in my bedroom closet. A few days later, I carried it outside and downstairs to the basement. I was going to bury him there, but I forgot that the cellar had a cement floor. There was an old trunk in the basement at the time and I put the bag in the trunk. I covered the trunk over with an old quilt that was in the trunk.

Q. What did the trunk look like?
A. Just an old trunk. I didn't really pay any attention to it.

Q. Where was the trunk in your basement?
A. It was up against the wall, the wall on the side where the water main is.

Q. Where is the trunk now?
A. Thrown out.

Q. When did the trunk get thrown out?
A. I took the bones out of it about four years after the fact. The trunk was thrown away anywhere from six months to two years after that.

Q. What did you do with the bones?
A. Some of them are up in my bedroom and those are the ones I found in the trunk.

Q. Where did you put the bones in your bedroom?
A. They are in a metal cabinet in my closet and the skull is in a brown file cardboard box on a metal stand in my room.

At this point, a shaken Childs looked at McVey who had a shocked look on his face. He then asked Norman if he would write a confession. Written on the confession sheet was a statement indicating that without coercion Norman had been advised of his rights to consult an attorney, could refuse to write such a statement because it could be used against him in court, and if he couldn't afford an attorney one would be provided for him.

Still shaking and twitching, Norman was ready to confess. He wrote the following in his scratchy handwriting:

"I was alone at home that Sunday and I saw Justin Doherty walking up the street. I had always thought it would be simple to kill someone and easy to get away with it and possibly fun in some way. I invited Justin into my house to look at a police pistol I said I had. We moved into my kitchen and I stabbed him in the chest from behind."

McVey took Norman's signed confession and quickly headed for Chief Velone's office.

"Chief, Norman Stedman has confessed to killing Justin Doherty. He says that he stabbed the boy and kept some of the boy's bones and his skull in his bedroom. Here's a copy of his signed statement."

As he sprung out of his chair, the chief's eyes lit up. He realized that breaking a high profile case like this one was a unique and sensational situation and would receive widespread media attention. And, having relegated Thurston to a secondary role, Velone now was in complete control of the investigation. He needed to take charge.

"Continue questioning Norman and get more information about possible evidence we might need to secure," he told McVey. "I want to talk with both you and Childs after you've finished. We need to get into the Stedman house as soon as possible and do a thorough search and seize all the evidence we can. And we need to move fast."

McVey returned to the conference room to privately update Childs before they resumed the interrogation. Norman appeared to have regained some of his composure as Childs began a new line of questioning.

Q. Do you know where the knife is that you used to kill Justin?
A. No, I don't. It was seven years ago; I doubt I still have it.

Q. Did you make any notes about what you had done?
A. I made notes a few years after the fact. The notes were in large part fictional. There was the basic fact of killing Justin; however, in the notes it says I choked him and had sex with him. I would like to submit to a lie detector test, because I have never had sex with any child.

Q. Where are the notes that you wrote?

A. In my bedroom, but I can't recall where they are.

Q. You say that the notes are fictional, except the part where you killed him. Is that the truth?
A. Yes. The notes start out saying something about the passage of time having passed over certain details and memory limitations caused embellishment of certain facts.

New beads of sweat formed on Norman's forehead. He started to shake again. He was concerned that the detailed notes describing his crime might severely damage his case. He wished he had destroyed them and not kept them as reminders of the pleasure he felt when he had Justin's dead body in his grasp.

When Childs paused in his questioning to allow for a break in the proceedings, Norman kept saying, "The notes are mainly fictional, they are fictional! Do you hear me! I was thinking about writing a play."

Chapter 29

After a break, Childs continued questioning Norman:

Q. After you killed Justin, did you take any of his clothes off?
A. Not at that time.

Q. How about later?
A. Yes, later when I got the bones, the clothes had decayed, falling off.

Q. Did you take anything off Justin at that time?
A. When I put him in the bag, I took off his shoes, because I was afraid they would poke a hole in the bag.

Q. What did you do with the shoes?
A. I put them in the trunk as well.

Q. Were the shoes thrown away with the trunk?
A. Yes.

Q. Did you keep anything that belonged to Justin, other than his bones?
A. No, I did not.

Q. Why did you keep the bones?
A. I didn't want to throw them away as they might be traced back to me.

Q. What do you mean traced back to you?
A. I was afraid that if I threw them in the garbage can, they would be knocked over by dogs, and they would be seen.

Q. When you kept the skull, did you keep the whole skull?

A. When I got the skull quite a number of teeth had dropped out of it and I couldn't find them.

Q. Are there any teeth left in the skull?
A. There are about four or five still left in it.

Q. Did you cut up the body at all before putting it into the plastic bag?
A. No, I did not.

Q. Did you put him in whole?
A. Yes, I did.

Q. Previous to having Justin come into your house that day had you had any other young kids in your house?
A. No.

Q. Have you killed any other persons or children?
A. No, I have not.

Q. When you killed Justin, did this come from your desire to just have fun?
A. No, not really. It was something inside of me. It's easy being someone else rather than yourself. It probably is one of the reasons why I went into theatre.

Q. Did you have any reason for doing this to Justin?
A. No, just random killing.

Q. If it had been some other kid walking up that street that day, would you have still done it?
A. Yes, it would not have necessarily been a kid.

Q. Did you have any anger or frustration at the time you did this?
A. The only thing I can say in regard to that is I have always seen myself on the outside of things. I have never been a part of anything or in with anyone. That's one of the reasons I don't have any close friends. I have friends, but no one that I can talk to about serious things.

Q. Is everything you said in this statement the truth?
A. Yes.

Q. Is there anything else you would like to add?
A. Yes. It's not easy asking for help when you're alone and you don't know whom to ask.

After Childs and McVey escorted Norman back to his cell, they immediately went to Chief Velone's office and were joined there by Rick Thurston. The chief was now very anxious to search the Stedman house, especially when he heard that Norman had apparently written his own description of the killing and included details about what he did with the dead boy's body. Childs and McVey reported that Norman had lied to them and was purposely slanting his testimony in order to discredit the damaging things he had written in his notes.

Thurston recommended that the chief get a search warrant as soon as possible. Velone disagreed, claiming it would take too much time and they needed to conduct the search now, not in two or three days. He wanted to approach Fred Stedman at his house and have him sign a "Consent to Search" statement, allowing the police to search the house immediately and seize valuable evidence.

Thurston worried that Norman's defense lawyers would use the lack of an official search warrant as a means to suppress crucial evidence later on in court. He also reasoned that although Fred Stedman owned the house, Norman was an adult and entitled to the privacy of his own bedroom. He insisted that a search warrant was the safest option.

Velone would hear none of it. Relying on his past investigative experience, he believed that in these circumstances the court would uphold any challenge by defense lawyers. He had successfully used written consent statements before and they were never questioned, and he didn't believe they would be in this case.

The next morning, the Richmonds visited the police station to talk with Officer McVey. Bud Richmond told him, "Donnie has more to add to the witness statement he gave you the other night."

McVey took Donnie and his parents to a small conference room and sat them at a small oak table. A harsh sunlight caused McVey to close the blinds before listening to what Donnie had to say.

Q. Hi, Donnie, how are you doing?
A. Ok, I guess.

McVey followed up, "I hear you want to add to your statement. Good, let me begin by asking you a few questions."

Q. On Thursday evening, April 15, 1982, did you give me, Officer Hal McVey, a statement at the Hopeville Police Station?
A. Yes, to Detective Childs and you.

Q. At this time do you wish to add to that statement?
A. Yes, when I went into Norman Stedman's house and up to his bedroom and before I had anything to drink, I saw a small skull. Norman said he got it from a play he was in. I then asked him if it was real and he said it was.

Q. During the time you were in Norman's house, do you remember ever having your clothes off at all?
A. No.

Q. Do you have anything further to state at this time concerning Norman?
A. Yes, every day that I delivered the paper to Norman, he would always tell me that if I ever came up for a drink not to bring my bike. He has asked me to come up for a drink for about six months or so saying that other kids my age had been drinking with him and I should too.

Q. Why didn't you tell Detective Childs on April 15, 1982, about the skull and bike?
A. That night it never entered my mind. It came to me a couple of days later when I started to recall things.

Donnie's information was old news. When the Richmonds left the station, McVey was amazed at how fast the whole murder case involving Norman was unfolding. The police had seized the skull, bones, and other critical evidence from the Stedman house the day before.

Chapter 30

Velone didn't even wait for Childs and McVey to complete their questioning of Norman when he heard they had a signed confession from Norman. Without a signed search warrant, he and Harrison immediately rushed to the Stedman residence at 18 Suffork Street knowing that crucial physical evidence of the crime was still in Norman's bedroom.

Norman's house was across the street about fifty yards down from Justin Doherty's house. It was a one and a half story dwelling with light green colored asbestos shingles and white trim. Gray cement steps with black iron handrails led to a worn looking green front door that desperately needed a fresh coat of paint. It was one of the old mill houses on the street and it looked very much the same as it had seventy years before. There was a cracked front window and the shades were pulled down.

Velone and Harrison walked up the cement steps and knocked on the door. Fred Stedman greeted them with a worried look on his face.

"What can I do for you fellows?"

Velone took the lead formally addressing Fred. "Mr. Stedman, we need to search your son's bedroom to recover some items he said were there that relate to Justin Doherty's disappearance."

With terrified look on his face, Fred muttered, "Chief, my house is a mess. I haven't cleaned it in awhile."

"That's all right; we are only going into Norman's bedroom. But before we enter your house, I need you to sign this Consent to Search form. Please read it first." Velone felt he needed to limit the search, because a broader search of the house that day might have legally jeopardized the need for a more thorough court approved search later on.

Without protest, Fred quickly read the form, took Velone's pen and signed it.

"Thank you. I want you to know that several other police officers will be joining us shortly to assist with the search."

Although appearing tense and perplexed, Fred was no stranger to police work and what a search by a number of police officers implied. He didn't know the new chief that well, but as a former active reserve policeman he did know most of the veteran Hopeville police officers, especially Rick Thurston, who he had gone on patrol with several times. He also maintained contact with several regular police officers, some of whom were his former colleagues.

The Hopeville police thought of Fred as a one of them. He was polite and friendly, but quiet and awkward socially. Although capable in the type of jobs he had held over the years, as Thurston put it, "He was not the brightest bulb on the Christmas tree, but a real nice guy." Fred had enjoyed his part time police work, but the chances of him ever becoming a regular police officer were slim.

Physically, he resembled his son but was smaller, cleaner and neater. In his police uniform he lacked the physical presence you would associate with an officer of the law. He was also too old at this point to apply for a full time police position.

Before Velone and Harrison began the house search, Thurston and Dr. Larry Biddle of the state medical examiners office arrived, and shortly thereafter, along with Jeff Childs who was now serving as police photographer. All parties put on coveralls and gloves and waded through the incredible pile of rubble that filled every room in the house. An article in the local paper described the scene, "As the men worked their way through the house, dirty clothes and assorted debris were everywhere, on the floor, piled on furniture, even scattered along the stairway to the second floor."

In all his years of police work, Velone said he had never seen such a filthy house. Thurston and Harrison were also shocked at what they saw as they carefully picked through the mess.

"I saw plates of uneaten food on the floor, stacks of old newspapers in every corner, underwear containing human feces just laying around and cat shit all over the place. It was awful," Thurston said.

Childs had some problems photographing the scene. "The litter was so bad that when I tried to take some shots inside the house, someone had to steady me as I stood on piles of clothes, magazines, newspapers, you name it."

Harrison distinctly remembered the offensive odor in the house. "It smelled rotten, obviously due to a number of things. The closest thing I can think of is the smell you get when there is a dead animal in your house."

Norman's grandmother had died in 1978 and his stepmother in 1980. The few people who did get inside the Stedman house reported that the house was not as bad while the two ladies lived there, but they did say that a pungent stench was present for many years before Justin was killed in 1975.

Thurston recalled driving Fred around in his cruiser when Fred was a reserve policeman in the late 1950's and 1960's. "Fred always smelled bad, almost like a garbage pail. It got so bad that I told my sergeant that I wouldn't take him on patrol in my cruiser any more."

A distant cousin of the Stedmans collected rubbish at Fred's house. He noticed that both Fred and his second wife spent a considerable amount of time sitting in their cars in their driveway reading paperbacks.

One time he asked Fred's mother, "Hey, why are they always sitting in their cars every time I do a pickup?"

"They can't stand the smell in the house, that's why," the feisty old lady answered.

How any one could stand the smell in the house and then carry the odor on their clothes and person was a mystery to those who knew Fred and Norman. Yet neither of them did anything about the problem and continued to let it negatively affect their relationships. Were they aware of it? Did they care? Were they incapable of getting rid of it? No one knew.

While police upstairs rummaged through his son's bedroom, Fred cornered Thurston in the downstairs living room. He had known Thurston for a long time, first meeting him in the local 4 H club years before. He trusted Thurston, and asked him, in a whisper, "Rick, did he do it?"

A saddened Thurston replied, "Fred, it doesn't look good."

Fred dropped to the floor, crying hysterically. Thurston, now joined by Harrison tried to console him, but couldn't. Finally, after they sat him down on a sofa, the tears stopped. His eyes looked glassy, as if he were in a trance. Thurston said, "I thought he had died."

Both Thurston and Harrison believed that Fred knew nothing about what Norman had done to Justin. They felt Norman was completely capable of manipulating and fooling his father. The policemen were also convinced that Norman's deceased stepmother and grandmother had been ignorant of Norman's criminal acts as well.

Harrison put it best, "I have seen fathers who, when having knowledge of their son's criminal activities, lie and become involved in a cover up. If you had witnessed Fred's sorrow and the raw anguish when Rick told him his son was a possible murderer, you would have seen that his reaction was genuine. The guy just didn't know.

"Quite simply Fred had never known what to do with Norman. He couldn't understand or control him especially after his mother and his second wife died. Norman was a smart kid and considerably more intelligent than Fred and he took advantage of him."

Meanwhile, Velone, medical examiner Biddle, and Childs were upstairs hoping to find some tangible evidence in Norman's bedroom.

Chapter 31

"Here it's over here!" Childs yelled.

He had lifted the cover off a cardboard box on Norman's bedroom bookshelf and found a small skull inside. A few teeth were still left in the mouth. Its shiny appearance suggested that it had probably been shellacked. Childs's body sagged. He looked as if he wanted to vomit.

Moments later, Medical Examiner Biddle opened a metal cabinet and inside were twenty-five bones, also apparently shellacked. Forensic consultants later confirmed that the bones represented about fifty percent of a small human skeleton.

The studious looking Biddle with his black horned rim glasses drooping to the tip of his generous nose carefully placed the bones in cloth bags with identification tags. The bones ranged from pelvic bones, tibia, and ribs to foot bones, kneecaps, and femur.

They had been deliberately stripped of all flesh, were unscarred and had not been exposed to the elements. Biddle concluded that the body, or at least parts of it, had been boiled, possibly in a weak lye solution and soap.

Detectives also seized other important evidence in Norman's bedroom that would later play a strategic role in his prosecution. In the bottom of the metal cabinet, several 18"x 12" sheets of paper were found with notes scribbled on them. In addition, there was a college examination blue book containing what looked like a narrative written in black ink. Writing experts later determined that it was Norman's writing. The notes scribbled on the sheets of paper appeared to have been written four or five years prior, while the writing in the blue book appeared to be more recent, no more than a year or so old.

The blue book apparently contained Norman's rambling account of how he had killed Justin. As newspapers hit the newsstands, rumors about the alleged contents of the blue book swirled around town. The rumors were quite explicit. The sketchy notes on the large paper sheets were used to write the narrative in the blue book. The blue book account reportedly detailed in grisly terms how Norman lured Justin into his house, stabbed him and then sexually violated his dead body before most of the remains, but not all, were disposed of in the town landfill.

After the skull and bones were seized and this information made public by the police, a reliable source supposedly leaked an "unspeakable piece of information" that, though unsubstantiated, still persists to this day. Norman had eaten parts of the boy's remains and performed sex on the dead boy. Although only the Superior Court judge, lawyers for the prosecution and defense, Chief Velone, Detectives Thurston and Harrison, and members of the state parole board actually read Norman's blue book narrative, the rumors about cannibalism and necrophilia quickly took on a life of their own. The Judge eventually sealed the infamous blue book from the media and Justin's family. It has been locked in Velone's office safe since 1982 and is now referred to by the police as "the sealed journal."

Norman, of course, vehemently denied having had sex with the dead boy or doing anything else with the remains except letting them decompose in a cellar trunk for four years.

"The contents of my narrative are mostly fictional and grossly embellished," he said over and over again. Norman viewed himself as a budding playwright. He claimed his ghastly account was but a summary of an original screenplay he was writing, a screenplay that someday would be celebrated by critics everywhere.

Other evidence found in his bedroom was both revealing and puzzling. Norman had kept several photocopies of local newspaper accounts of Justin's disappearance and the search that followed. A one pint empty bottle of Smirnoff Vodka was taken from the top bureau drawer. Two knives in leather sheaths and a pocketknife were seized from the top section of a white metal cabinet. One sex aid, a small notebook containing the name Ruby Nile, a man's brown billfold and four metal canisters containing film were also seized. The film was later found to be family movies. All of these items were placed in cloth bags with bag numbers written on identification tags.

One piece of seized evidence in particular puzzled investigators. In the right hand top drawer of the bedroom dresser, two needles and syringes and one vial of Foradil and one vial of Tubocurarine chloride were found. A toxicology test confirmed that Foradil was a long-acting bronchodilator that relaxes muscles in the airways to improve breathing. It can be used to treat symptoms of nighttime asthma and obstructive pulmonary diseases such as emphysema and chronic bronchitis. It is critical for a person to use it in the prescribed dosage or it can increase the risk of asthma related death.

Tubocurarine chloride is a drug to paralyze patients undergoing anesthesia. Used actively in the 1970's to "knock people out" before surgery, it has since fallen into disuse in western medicine; however, it is still used in the United States and elsewhere as part of the lethal injection procedure.

What were these drugs doing in Norman's bedroom? Where did he get them? Had he used them on anyone? Why was his stepmother's illness so prolonged? Was it just Vodka that caused Donnie Richmond to pass out for such an unusually long time on the kitchen floor? Police did not seek answers to these questions. They had enough evidence to prosecute Norman once they had his written confession and now his journal.

It is unlikely Norman personally used the drugs for any medical problems. He was not asthmatic and was constantly seen walking everywhere in town—to the library, the high school, the village green, the college or work. No asthmatic could walk as many miles as he did each day. With his large body slumped over beneath a full backpack, he constantly plodded around town. People who had close contact with him, like his teachers and theatre acquaintances, never noticed him experiencing any difficulty breathing. The only reason he may have had for injecting himself was to experience temporary euphoric escape from his painful existence.

Norman worked as an orderly at Hopeville Hospital where drugs were accessible, usually sitting in a hospital cart after surgery when Norman remained to clean the operating room and wash the surgical instruments. Unlike today, in the 1970's, drugs used in hospitals were not kept under lock and key. Norman may have also snitched other drugs from the hospital beside the two seized by police. One hospital official wondered if he might even have taken some Valium, since it was used frequently and was openly accessible in the operating room.

One can only speculate as to why Norman had the drugs in his possession. Was it simply morbid curiosity? Was he planning to inject possible future victims and make them unconscious before he sexually violated them? Did he inject the family cat with one of the drugs? More specifically, did he slip one of the drugs into the Vodka he gave to the boys he invited into his bedroom for a drink?

Reportedly, his black cat went wild on him one day, attacking him and scratching his face as it flew around his bedroom. The cat eventually had to be put away, because of its abnormal behavior. All this of course is just conjecture. Only Norman knows the real answers to these questions, questions no one ever asked him.

After the police completed the search, a neighbor saw the medical examiner and his assistant emerge from the house carrying a stretcher out to their van. She was relieved because she had seen the stretcher wheeled in an hour before and thought someone had died. She didn't give much thought to the two large shopping bags the two men were carrying until she heard the news about Justin.

"When they told me it might have been Justin I almost fainted," she said.

Chapter 32

Immediately after Norman's confession and before his arrest was publicly acknowledged by the police and the media, Velone called the Dohertys and asked them to meet with him in his office. He said he had some very important information to share with them.

Upon arriving they sat silently in the lobby for several minutes waiting to see Velone. When Thurston learned they were downstairs, he immediately went to greet them and quietly told them it was better if they got the news about Justin from Velone rather than from him. Before he could say another word, Velone appeared and escorted the two nervous parents to his upstairs office.

Velone explained how he had the sad responsibility of reporting the resolution of their son's case. He purposely did not refer to the horror of the murder, but simply stated the general facts surrounding the arrest of Norman Stedman. The only quote he gave to the press was that George and Jane were "Most naturally saddened at the news." Recalling the scene in later years, he described it in greater detail, "The parents, in hearing the news, were stunned and in a state of mild shock. Their heads went down and their bodies went limp. No one spoke for a long, long time."

After they left Velone, Thurston asked Jane and George to come into his office. There, the stricken parents embraced and quietly sobbed in one another's arms. After almost seven years, Thurston had a special relationship with them, particularly Jane.

"I had told Jane to be prepared for the worst and hope for the best. I thought she would be prepared, but she wasn't," he said. "She had no doubt in her mind that we'd find the little guy. I don't know how they lived with it for so long, the burden of not knowing. At least they now knew, but that was no consolation.

"This is like the kind of thing you read about happening in New

York City, a tabloid story. We've never had this kind of thing before. People in town were both angry and frightened."

Newspaper stories reported how Thurston worked, ate and slept the case for all those years, how he checked every conceivable lead. While others scoffed, he listened and accepted help from psychics, astrologists, hypnotists, and amateur sleuths. He traveled out of state to schools to check out newly enrolled youngsters who matched Justin's description down to the pockmark on his nose and the small gap between his two front teeth. The week before Norman confessed, he was packing his bags to go to Virginia to interview another relative of Jane's. "I wanted to make sure I didn't miss anything," he said.

Chief Velone publicly commended the detectives for their "bread and butter police work and diligence over a long period of time." The "bread and butter" police work in this case unfortunately reinforced what every rookie cop knows. So often, it's right in front of your nose, but you don't see it.

Chapter 33

The headlines in the local, state and national papers told it all. "Justin: Macabre, Grisly Writings Tell of Perfect Crime." "How Could Police Have Missed House?" "Diary-like Statement Reportedly Links Suspect to Justin Doherty's Slaying." "A Whole Community Has Been Shaken."

Over that weekend, Norman underwent psychiatric examination at the Institute of Mental Health (IMH) in Boston. He was scheduled for arraignment the following morning in Hopeville District Court.

Thurston and Harrison sat directly in back of Norman in the courtroom when he was arraigned. Thurston said he had heard rumblings like the one from a local man who said, "Somebody should shoot that bastard if they get a chance." Others were saying, "He almost killed two kids. If the Richmond kid hadn't come to, he would have been a goner. That guy is sick and needs to be put away permanently."

Although it was only talk, Thurston admitted that anger was widespread in town. "As we sat there in back of Norman in court, believe me, I thought about some crazy sniper or Jack Ruby type putting a bullet into Norman's head. The hostility felt toward Norman and the inhuman thing he had done was running high, very high."

Norman stood expressionless during his six-minute arraignment for the murder of five-year-old Justin Doherty. The Judge ordered the preliminary psychiatric evaluation of Norman done at the Institute of Mental Health (IMH) in Boston sealed. A source familiar with the case said the report pronounced the suspect competent to stand trial. He also agreed to return Norman to the IMH for a neurological assessment.

A Springfield newspaper reporter described the court scene:

"The courtroom fell silent as sheriff's deputies led Norman Stedman in from a cell in the basement where he had been staying waiting for the arraignment to begin. During a short recess, Detective Captain Rick

Thurston, who spent years searching for Justin's abductor, walked over to the suspect's gray-haired father, touched his arm and whispered to him."

Asked later what he said, the Rick replied, "I just wanted to calm him down. I've known him for a long time. This is tough."

Seated besides the elder Stedman was Pastor Hobson, who said later that he had been spending time with his parishioner over the last few days to show him that we are supportive and concerned.

When approached, Pastor Hobson explained, "Fred is very active in our church and has been a deacon for years. I didn't know his son at all until I met him recently. My role is to give Fred all the support I can. He is a gentle man and although somewhat passive, he is shocked and stunned by his son's arrest." Hobson would later accompany Fred when he visited Norman at the IMH and in prison.

Fred wasn't the only one "shocked and stunned." The local paper reported that residents of Hopeville were struggling with "feelings of disbelief, anger, sympathy and fear" as the mystery of what had happened to Justin Doherty appeared to be over after seven years.

A local newspaper article contained this summary, *Disbelief that despite all their prayers, Justin is dead. Anger that a neighbor, a native son of this close knit semi-rural town is charged with murdering a five-year-old boy. Residents felt sympathy for the Dohertys and Fred Stedman, who grieve privately for their sons, and fear that someday it could happen to them.*

"I think the best way to describe it is numbness," said one prominent political figure who grew up a street over from Norman's house.

"People had always thought Justin was kidnapped, not murdered in the way police believe he was. I worry about how this will affect our relationships with people who aren't in our own families. There will be a tendency to distrust strangers and anyone who seems different, even our own neighbors."

A mother of young children, who knew Norman when they both were cast in the same Community Players production, underscored the need to fight a breakdown in community trust. "We're all wounded by this. There isn't a mother in this town whose heart is not broken for Mrs. Doherty. This community is going to have to heal itself and take this opportunity to become better. It won't be easy, but you have to go beyond this, you have to trust people."

The minister of the local congregational church talked about the need for closure. "I find that people need to express their concern and their love for the Doherty family in order to bring his whole thing into focus and to a close."

Chapter 34

Velone sat in his soft brown leather office chair deep in thought. It had been two days since Norman had been arrested and arraigned in Hopeville District Court and he knew the high profile case would totally consume his department in the weeks and months ahead. His detectives would have little time to attend to other business, given the need for compiling evidence to support a grand jury indictment and then a trial.

Things were indeed getting complicated. The physical evidence seized in the Stedman house, especially Norman's writings in the journal, would have to be submitted to the grand jury. Rumor had it that the public defender, John Kenny, who had been assigned to represent Norman, would be requesting a delay in the grand jury hearing, claiming it should convene in another county because of the adverse local publicity the case had received. However, a call to a court official by Velone indicated that Kenny had not yet filed a motion to move the session to another county.

In any event, the chances of having a grand jury hearing by the end of April or early May were diminishing by the minute. It looked as if the evidence wouldn't be ready for a grand jury hearing before the end of June, which meant that a return of an indictment probably wouldn't come until late August.

The state attorney general was quoted as saying that his department would prosecute Norman as an adult for first degree murder despite the fact that he had been only sixteen in 1975 when he said he killed Justin, "We don't feel the Family Court has jurisdiction over a twenty-three-year-old man." His opinion was based upon research done by his staff on crimes committed by juveniles who were not arrested until they were over twenty-one. Although there were no Massachusetts cases involving decisions of this nature, similar decisions in other jurisdictions strongly supported the decision to try Norman as an adult in Superior Court rather than as a juvenile in Family Court.

The case against Norman was further complicated by the difficulty Medical Examiner Biddle had in confirming that the bones found by the police were in fact Justin's. Biddle was working at a disadvantage in having only twenty-five bones, a fraction of the complete skeleton. Many of his usual methods of consulting dental records, x-rays, and other medical records were not applicable to this case because Justin was only five-years-old and didn't have a sufficient medical history. He also was in generally good health, according to his local physician.

Biddle contacted Harrison and asked him to ask Jane Doherty for further information about Justin's height, weight, clothing size, and any childhood illnesses he may have had.

Jane told Harrison that Justin had chicken pox in 1971 and it took him awhile to get over it. This detail coincided with Biddle's initial examination of the bones, in which he detected evidence of a childhood illness of measles or chicken pox. Jane also reported that her son was three feet or greater, weighed about forty pounds or slightly more, and had a clothing size of six to eight in boys' pants and medium to tall in boys' shirts.

Because Justin still had all his baby teeth, his dentist had not listed his teeth on a chart or taken any x-rays. Jane also wanted Biddle to know that Justin had been a thumb sucker since he was six weeks old.

At a press conference, his deputy and an orthopedic surgeon joined Biddle and reported their preliminary findings. "There is nothing to indicate at this point that we are not dealing with Justin's remains. Because the boy was so young and the fact there are no medical records we can't say, and probably will never be able to say, that this is the young man with a one hundred percent certainty of being right."

The medical examiner did however have Justin's blood type. After getting a written release from Jane, his office contacted the medical records division at Norfolk General Hospital and learned that his blood type was A-positive. A blood test is usually not done on newborns, but in Justin's case it was because of a question concerning the RH-Factor of the parents.

Biddle also wanted a stuffed blue and green toy seal that Justin took to bed with him each night and an electric hair clipper in the hope of finding hair samples. He asked Jane to provide Harrison with as many photos of Justin as she could locate.

The stuffed toy seal, the hair clipper, and the five knives seized by police from Norman's house were sent to the FBI laboratory for analysis. The photos showed that Justin slept on his left side, which indicated that he probably sucked his right thumb. This information, along with other tests conducted by forensic experts would be most helpful in the coming weeks. Biddle's strategy was to collect enough evidence beyond the graphic details recorded in Norman's bluebook to be used as evidence for the grand jury and later at a trial. His objective was to increase the degree of probability that the bones seized in Norman's bedroom were Justin's.

Velone was getting restless. So many questions and details relating to the case were swarming around in his head. He stared blankly out his office window and noticed a string of crocuses poking their little white and yellow heads through the muddy soil along the front entrance of the police station. It was April in the Berkshires, a time of growth, of newness.

He thought about the Dohertys, the Richmonds and Fred Stedman. All of them bound together by a brutal act of violence. How do the victims of such an awful, horrible, heinous crime of this nature ever cope and go on with their lives? He didn't have any answers, but his heart went out to them.

Velone buzzed his secretary. "Darlene, could you call Fred Stedman and ask him if he could meet with me tomorrow afternoon? Tell him I would like to take a statement from him. Hey, forget that. I'll call him myself."

Chapter 35

The next afternoon, Fred Stedman was pacing back and forth in the lobby of the police station waiting for Chief Velone to arrive. He had no idea what questions Velone might ask, but was quite apprehensive because he had heard that the Chief was a tough interrogator. This was not like the old days, when the police were his buddies. Velone didn't really know him or appreciate the solid reputation he had earned as a reserve policeman. "What will this guy ask me?" Fred thought as he felt sweat form under his armpits. " Does he think I knew that my son had murdered Justin? Is he questioning me because he's thinking of charging me as an accomplice?"

Upstairs in his office, Velone again called Thurston and Harrison telling him they were certain that Fred knew nothing about his son murdering Justin. Fred was supposedly shocked and broke down completely when he heard that Norman had confessed to the crime. Thurston had known Fred for years and was convinced that Fred was genuinely fooled by his son and had no clue about Norman being the killer. Velone wondered, however, if Thurston might have been blinded because of his past relationship with Fred.

Although it was something he didn't look forward to doing, Velone had to talk candidly to Fred about what he knew and what he didn't know. Everything Velone knew about Fred was secondhand. Although the reports were generally good, some people thought that Fred was a bit odd—not too different in personality from Norman. He felt a responsibility to personally question him to find out if Fred was indeed a victim and had not covered up for his son during the past few years. He might also gather other important facts about the case, facts that could prove helpful in gathering new evidence for later use in court.

Velone greeted Fred and brought him to the conference room to begin the questioning. There were no other witnesses in the room. Velone could tell Fred was uneasy so he tried to relax him by asking him about his time as a reserve policeman then, after a friendly exchange, got down to business.

Q. How long have you lived at 18 Suffork Street?
A. About twenty years.

Q. In May, 1975 who lived at 18 Suffork Street?
A. My mother, my second wife Dorothy, and my son Norman.

Q. Was your son a student in May of 1975?
A. I believe he was enrolled in Hopeville High School at that time.

Q. What is your son's full name?
A. Norman E. Stedman.

Q. What is your occupation presently?
A. Custodian at the Woodward Elementary School.

Q. How long have you been employed in your current job?
A. I retired from Berkshire Electric before I went to work as a custodian in September 1974.

Q. So is it a fair statement to say that you were employed in your current job in May of 1975?
A. Yes.

Q. Is Norman your only child?
A. My only living child at this time.

Q. Do you in your own knowledge remember the Justin Doherty missing person case in May 1975?
A. Yes. It was a Sunday. I was visiting my second wife's mother in Springfield during the afternoon and we came home around 7 p.m.

Q. Who went with you to visit your mother-in-law?
A. Just my wife Dorothy and myself.

Q. Where was your mother at the time?
A. My mother was visiting my sister who lives on Elmgrove Avenue in Hopeville.

Q. Is your mother still alive?
A. No sir.

Q. Did your son Norman ever tell you that he killed Justin Doherty?
A. No sir.

Q. During the course of time since May 18, 1975, did you observe within your home assorted newspapers in your son's possessions or in his room relating to the Justin matter?
A. I never went into his room. The first time I ever saw any articles was yesterday when you took them from his room. He used to get mad if anyone went into his room.

Q. Did there come a time between May 16, 1975, and this April when your cellar at 18 Suffork Street was cleaned up?
A. On at least two occasions I cleaned up part of it and then Irvin Hathaway cleaned it up for me.

Q. What is your best recollection as to when you partially cleaned your cellar?
A. I think it was after 1978 because I got a new truck at the time.

Q. When did Irvin Hathaway clean out your cellar?
A. It was after that I think, maybe in 1979. I paid Irvin twenty-five dollars to clean it out. He took the furnace out and the junk in the cellar at that time.

Q. Do you recall after May 18, 1975, ever seeing a trunk or box in your cellar?
A. There were two trunks in my cellar. One had a round type top and the other was square or rectangle.

Q. Did either Mr. Hathaway or you discard these two trunks when you cleaned out the cellar?
A. I think I took both trunks out and took them to the dump.

Q. Do you remember ever looking into the trunks before you discarded them?
A. Yes, the rectangle trunk was empty and the one with the rounded cover or top just appeared to have a quilt or cover inside it.

Q. Did the trunk with the rounded top that contained a quilt or cover have any smell to it?
A. Yes, it did but I thought that it was mildew or musty.

Q. Did you look under the quilt inside the trunk before you discarded it?
A. No.

Q. Did you observe any bones or flesh inside this trunk?
A. No sir.

Q. Did there come a time after you discarded these two trunks that you observed a skull and some bones in the bedroom of your son?
A. The first time I saw the skull and bones was about a month ago in his bedroom.

Q. Which bedroom is this?
A. The bedroom that you searched yesterday.

Q. Where exactly did you see the skull?
A. I saw it on top of a box on a gray metal bookcase in his room.

Q. Please describe the box that the skull was on top of?
A. It was a brown cardboard box.

Q Did you at any time observe any bones in your son's bedroom about that same time?
A. I think it was about the same time. The bones were where you found them yesterday. They were there when I first saw them in my son's bedroom.

Q. At any time after you observed the skull and bones in your son's bedroom did you have a conversation with your son Norman relative to these bones?
A. I asked him what the skull was doing in his bedroom. He told me that it was prop for a play. I knew he had been in a play not too long before that, but I didn't see that play so I believed him.

Q. Did you likewise ask him about the bones?
A. He told me they were also props for the play.

Q. Was there any doubt that he was being truthful about the skull and bones?
A. I had no reason to doubt him. He has been involved in many plays and I believed him. I remember him saying to me that every play he was in he always kept something as a souvenir.

Q. You earlier mentioned that you at one time gave a Charlie Ryan some articles of furniture from your cellar. Do you recall when this was?
A. It was after I went to the dump with the two trunks.

Q. You didn't give him one of the trunks?
A. No.

Q. Have you seen your son Norman in your house in the company of young boys?
A. A couple of years ago I remember he had a couple of parties but the people who came appeared to be about his age.

Q. Is there anything else you wish to add to this statement?
A. No, other than at one time Norman worked at Hopeville Hospital in the operating room as an orderly. I remember asking him if blood bothered him. He answered that it did not.

Q. Will you read these questions and your answers and tell me if your answers are true.
A. Yes, they are true.

Chapter 36

Velone escorted Fred back to the lobby and thanked him for his statement. He noticed that Fred had large black circles under his eyes and wondered if he had gotten any sleep during the past few days.

Looking at Fred's body, he wondered how he would physically describe him. He thought "pear shaped" would fit. Although he had a faintly noticeable body odor, Fred had pleasant facial features and was neat and clean-shaven in contrast to his son. Velone thought asking Fred for his statement was no big deal, just good routine police work. He was impressed with Fred's candid responses—the comment about Norman not being bothered by blood was an illustration—but also found Fred lacking in perspective, natural curiosity and intellectual depth. Fred was a simple man who did the best he could to try to understand a son who was very complex, shrewd, and intelligent. It was not surprising to the chief that Norman had kept Fred in the dark as long as he had and manipulated him so easily.

Norman was an obedient, polite, soft-spoken child who cleverly disguised the burning anger and rage inside him. At times that anger surfaced with his father and other family members. He simply wanted his family to leave him alone, keep out of his bedroom, and give him privacy. As Norman got older, he got upset and heated when they didn't and they usually backed down after facing his wrath. It's very conceivable that they didn't have any idea about the bizarre thoughts rumbling around in his head, nor did they have any knowledge of the grisly souvenirs he kept in his bedroom.

Of course, there were neighbors and townspeople who didn't agree with the police assessment of Fred as a truthful, shaken father. They had difficulty believing that Norman could live with his father, stepmother, and grandmother for a number of years in a house with an increasingly putrid smell without one of them becoming suspicious of his activities.

How could he boil the body, discard parts of it in the town landfill and then shellac the skull and bones without detection?

Neighbors remembered Norman and Fred sitting for hours in the car in their driveway and talking. They wondered if the discussions were connected to Fred's complicity in the murder of Justin.

One neighbor said, "Fred was a lot shrewder than the police thought he was. He had to know."

A veteran Hopeville policeman who knew Fred well said, "I never trusted Fred and felt he covered up for Norman. His emotional upset was not so much due to the shock of learning Norman had murdered Justin, but more about now realizing that his only son would be put away for the rest of his life. It was that reality that broke him up.

"I know this is conjecture on my part, but if your only son was all messed up and had committed murder would you turn him in? Wouldn't you try to convince him to turn himself in? Was Fred attempting to get Norman to surrender to the police during their extensive car conversations and getting nowhere because Norman was resisting coming forward? Apparently, Norman had other plans. He wanted to stay out of jail, kill again and didn't care whether he was caught or not. In fact, maybe he wanted to get caught."

It is unlikely that the long talks in the car had anything to do with the murder of Justin. Fred was never directly asked about those talks but he clearly indicated in his statement that he knew nothing about what Norman did to Justin until the arrest.

In his response to a question by Childs, Norman had stated that he had nobody with whom he could discuss serious matters. His shyness and low self-esteem made it difficult for him to carry on meaningful conversations with peers and adults. In fact, he had to bribe people to spend time with him. Norman wanted to, but simply couldn't confide in people, including, most likely, his father.

The car also provided Fred and Norman refuge from the terrible stench in the house, as it had for Fred and his wife. This stench got increasingly worse in the late 1970's, especially in Norman's bedroom. Velone asked Harrison to follow up with Irvin Hathaway, who Fred said had cleaned out his cellar. Hathaway was a crusty, tough-talking old carpenter who did odd jobs around town. He was questioned and his statements were consistent with Fred's testimony.

"I was asked to do work in his son's bedroom but I refused to do it. It stunk so badly. I told him to get the room cleaned out. The smell was just fricken awful.".

When Hathaway was asked what type of smell he detected he said, "I have never smelled anything like that before. It smelled like something was rotten. The whole time I worked in the house the door to that bedroom was never open. I did open the door one time but I closed it right up as I couldn't stand the smell."

Very few people entered Norman's bedroom. If he didn't keep everyone out, the smell did. His success in keeping his father, stepmother and grandmother out of his room may be the major reason they never had a clue about his being Justin's killer. However, there was one workman who did get inside Norman's bedroom in the late 1970's——the local electrician, Peter Jacobson. Peter tells an interesting story:

"I was called to do some work in Fred's house. He needed some wall lights put in. When I arrived, Fred, his wife, and Norman greeted me. I didn't see the grandmother but she might have been there.

"After I put the wall light in the kitchen, I went to Norman's bedroom to put a light in near his bedroom dresser. The room smelled like cat shit. I remember that the top drawer of the dresser was slightly open and I actually saw cat feces in the drawer and later on the floor. There was also a tiny bone in the drawer, but it didn't look like a human bone but more like a small chicken bone. My recollection about these things made me shiver when I learned a few years later that Norman murdered the boy and kept some of his bones.

"All the time while I was in his bedroom, Norman was at my side watching me intently.

"My general impression was that the whole house smelled, but Norman's bedroom really stunk. It was terrible."

Jacobson was asked later why he didn't wonder about the smell or at least mention it to someone else. He said, "I didn't make any connection with Stedman and the Doherty boy. I just thought it was just cat shit, because the shit was all around the room and hadn't been picked up."

The house had an offensive smell long before Norman killed Justin, but now it was obscenely rotten. The smell that penetrated his clothes had intensified. Obviously, his clothes had come in contact with decomposed body parts.

Chapter 37

At the end of May, Chuck Harrison met Dr. Biddle and other medical personnel in the medical examiner's office in Boston to review the procedures that would be used to gain a more positive identification of Justin's remains.

In addition to the information provided by Jane Doherty, Biddle wanted copies of any x-rays of family members' skulls or backs and reports of any family back problems. He also suggested that the police check the kitchen floor of the Stedman house to see if they could locate any traces of blood.

The team Biddle had formed to examine Justin's remains included a prominent Boston dentist, Dr. Glenn Gatliff, who specialized in dentistry for children and young adults; Dr. Clyde Winter, a forensic anthropologist from Oklahoma who had helped law enforcement officials throughout the country identify human remains; Dr. Hilson Jones, a director of forensic pathology in Toronto who had a high success rate in making identifications and obtaining convictions with a system he developed using television cameras to make super-impositions rather than clay models; and Dr. Albert Dodenberg of the University of Chicago, an expert in comparing similarities of dental bone structures among family members.

Two other national consultants performed isotope tests to determine time of death, and if need, be to examine the bones to determine blood type. Although DNA testing was not available in the early 1980's, the medical examiner's office and the Hopeville police spared no expense in hiring the very best forensic experts in the country to examine the remains found in Norman's bedroom. Before they presented evidence to a jury, they wanted to be as certain as possible that those remains were indeed Justin Doherty's.

Detectives Harrison and Monroe were sent on details to Chicago and Toronto, carrying the skull and bones and all photos and negatives of Justin back and forth on each trip.

Biddle and the Hopeville police worked closely with Assistant Attorney General Linda McCaffrey, who was assigned as prosecutor in Justin's case. McCaffrey was particularly concerned with transporting critical evidence throughout the country and into Canada and wanted to insure that it was carefully handled and accounted for at all times. She was not at the meeting in Biddle's office when taking the key evidence out of state was discussed, but she did leave instructions that the remains should not be taken out of state until she returned from vacation.

They decided not to submit Norman's writing for expert analysis at that time, fearing that there was too high a risk of damage being done in the handling and analysis of the paperwork. If they needed an expert analysis, it could be done later.

Dr. Gatliff concluded that based upon the measurements of the dentition and examination of the x-rays, the skull appeared to be that of a male child approximately five years of age in good general health and without significant dental disease. The condition of the remaining teeth suggested an active thumb sucker but was not definitive.

Dr. Dodenburg supported Dr. Gatliff's findings. His examination revealed that the finger-like projection on the incisors plus the irregularity of the surfaces of the remaining teeth were compatible with those of other family members. His estimate of the probability of the combination of events he observed repeating ranged close to 64,000 or more to one.

Dr. Winter concluded that the remains came from a single human skeleton. Their condition indicated that the body decomposed naturally in some type of protected environment. The bones were not obtained commercially. The time of death was determined scientifically to have occurred between four and twenty years prior to the remains being discovered.

His examination further revealed that the remains were those of a white male with light blond, straight hair, approximately five years old, between forty-three and forty-eight inches tall, and weighing approximately forty-six pounds. Winter stated that in his professional opinion, the remains were those of Justin Doherty.

Dr. Jones's examination of the super-imposition revealed a ninety percent probability that the skull was Justin Doherty's.

The results of the chemical analysis done at the FBI laboratory also arrived. The five knives sent for analysis were examined for the presence of blood but none was found.

As a result, the murder weapon was never found. Norman's response to the question of what type of knife he used to kill Justin, "It was a kitchen knife, but I'm not sure" was all the police had to go on.

Velone obtained a search warrant for the purposes written in his request, "to search for any human remains such as bones, bone chips or fragments of dried blood, flesh, or hairs located within any room of the dwelling on 18 Suffork Street." The search was specifically focused on the floors of the house and any sub flooring or floor covering.

Detectives Harrison and Childs joined Thurston in checking all rooms in the Stedman house. The house had been cleaned up considerably since the first search had been conducted, except for Norman's bedroom which looked just like it did the day they arrested him. A local contractor also joined the detectives to remove the kitchen floor covering along with some pieces of stained wallpaper. It was impossible to retrieve the old pink tile base floor in the kitchen to get blood specimens, because a covering installed in 1978 was glued right to it.

When they learned of the attempt to locate blood specimens for testing, Dr. Biddle and Dr.Winter agreed that blood testing on the family and the remains should not be done at this time. They felt that the tests conducted to date had shown with a great degree of certainty that the remains were Justin's, and further blood testing might have varying degrees of error and possibly jeopardize the case.

Biddle was very pleased, however, with the positive results of the hair analysis done by Dr. Winter. Winter had clearly matched the blond hair found on the skull with traces of hair found on Justin's stuffed toy seal and hair clippers. Biddle and Attorney McCaffrey believed that these conclusive results and the medical reports done by their consultants would be enough for the grand jury to indict Norman. They agreed to submit the case to the grand jury by the first of July.

That August the grand jury returned an indictment against Norman E. Stedman for the murder of five-year-old Justin Doherty.

Chapter 38

Public Defender John Kenny had a problem. His client, Norman Stedman, had been indicted for murder and had given an oral and written confession to the police. There was also damaging physical evidence against him. Furthermore, state psychiatrists had declared Norman competent for trial, said he was highly intelligent, and, although lonely and nervous, not delusional. An insanity defense would be fruitless. Clearly, Norman was facing a life sentence, the maximum penalty under state law. Somehow, this respected public defender with a handsome face and likeable demeanor had to convince state prosecutor Linda McCaffrey that a plea bargain would be in everybody's best interest.

John Kenny tried for months to get Linda to negotiate a plea bargain. He liked her and had worked cooperatively with her in the past. She was a rising star in the judicial world, determined and even aggressive when she had to be. She also could be stubborn. She steadily refused Kenny's request for a plea bargain, respecting the wishes of the Dohertys and the Richmonds to put Norman away forever, as she had promised to do.

"The madman deserves to rot in prison" was the feeling among the families of the victims and just about everybody else in town.

Norman's journal in the blue book, which allegedly graphically described what he did to Justin's body, was Kenny's only trump card. After reading it, he knew that making the argument that Norman's account was mainly fictional would not work. Norman would not escape a life sentence and maybe even get life without parole. Kenny realized his first responsibility as a public defender was to his client, and that the sensational publicity releasing the contents of the journal would generate would affect Norman's ability to survive in prison. He also hoped that Linda would realize that releasing the contents of the journal would be devastating to Justin's family.

Linda refused to consider a plea bargain throughout the fall of 1982, but when she and John began meeting again after the first of the year she eventually agreed to talk to the Dohertys and Richmonds about their feelings on the matter.

The *Hopeville Times* provided an explanation of what happened next:

John Kenny began meeting with Norman Stedman on Sunday mornings at the prison explaining the options. They faced each other in blue plastic chairs, trying to determine the best deal Stedman could get so he didn't have to spend the rest of his life in prison.

Linda McCaffrey, in turn, met with the Dohertys and the Richmonds. The Richmonds were worried that a trial would have their son on a witness stand, reliving his ordeal. The Dohertys were torn. They wanted the justice Linda McCaffery had promised, but they also wanted to end their terrible nightmare.

Step by step, McCaffrey and Kenny proceeded, consulting with their clients at intervals to seek permission to continue talking. Talks intensified with Kenny meeting with his client four more times.

As the trial date neared, defense and prosecution attorneys approached the man who would have to approve the bargain they were shaping, Judge Walter Griffin, who met separately with the families involved to explain the issues and to get an assurance that no one objected to the plea bargain, including Norman.

In the end, all parties—the police department, the attorneys, the attorney general, the judge and both families—officially approved the plea bargain. The charge against Norman was changed from first degree to second-degree murder. He was sentenced to fifty years in prison with ten years suspended. He would have to wait at least fifteen years before being considered for parole.

The attorney general and assistant attorney general felt they gained solace for the Dohertys and now ran no risk of Norman being acquitted. Although Norman had no guarantee of parole, Kenny thought that forty years in prison was better than life. Judge Griffin, in accepting the agreement carved out by the two attorneys, said, 'The bargain was in the best interests of the defendant and of those who mourn, and those who suffer.

Chapter 39

With the case now completed, Justin's remains were returned to his family. The Dohertys arranged what the minister called "a closing service" at the Hopeville Congregational Church. As Reverend Bruce Foster, the pastor and elder statesman of the 125-year-old church publicly explained, "This service is something this troubled town needs to express their concern and their love for the Doherty family and to bring the whole thing into focus and to a close. It will be a chance to ask what is the meaning in our faith and in our lives."

The church's 375-seat sanctuary was packed with the media. Television trucks had rolled up and reporters scurried about attempting to get their thirty-second blip for the evening news and grist for their stories in the next edition of their newspapers.

Jane and George and their two remaining children were seated in the semi-darkness of the church. Jane was gently wiping away her tears during the emotional service. When she stood with the congregation for the closing hymn, she crumbled, burying her head and her sobs in George's chest as he steadied her.

The focal point of the service was a small alabaster coffin trimmed in gold, crowned with a pink-and-blue bouquet, and flanked by two flickering tapers.

Pastor Foster spoke first, "I believe that Justin has been cared for by the angels of Heaven and now at this point in his growth, he is probably more ready to help us than we him."

Nearly seven years before, Foster had stood in front of the same altar, after Justin had been missing for a week, and said, "I hope that someone has him and will release him to the family soon. If he is no longer alive, then he is ready to go home."

Sitting close to the Dohertys at the closing service was Rick Thurston, whose commitment to them in seven long years of searching for their son was an example of dedication rarely seen from law officials.

It was Rick's turn to step into the pulpit to speak for the community and talk about a "new beginning." As he tried to speak he choked up and was unable to read the text he had labored over earlier in the week.

Instead, he haltingly delivered a simpler message: "George and Jane, I just know that happiness must come from this time on—and God will see to it."

A few minutes later, Pastor Foster looked out at the congregation and asked them to join him in the singing of "Hymn 195." He said it was a resurrection hymn. "Let us sing it to the glory of God in memory of Justin." People joined hands and sang together and the tears flowed.

PART TWO

Chapter 40

It was the summer of 1982 shortly after Norman's arrest. Gary Thomas was waiting in the lobby of the Hopeville Police Station to see Chief of Police, Paul Velone. The pale blue lobby was separated from the dispatcher's office by a sliding glass window and behind it sat several uniformed policemen chatting as they sipped their morning coffee. On the lobby wall, Gary noticed a row of faded pictures of old, retired police buildings and formal, serious looking pictures of former chiefs dating back to Hopeville's first, Harvey Suffork. "Those Sufforks seem to be everywhere," he thought.

A honey oak trophy case also caught his eye. Inside the case were written citations, framed photographs, and plaques given over the years to Hopeville policemen for professional achievements. Gary smiled as he saw two plaques that had been given to Rick Thurston commending him for going beyond the call of duty.

Rick was always a hell raiser in his youth and beyond, while Gary was younger, and one of those studious types that never got out of line. Handsome and personable Rick was what the girls called "a hot throb"—a label that didn't bother him at all. In spite of their differences, Gary had always liked Rick and was happy to see that he had found his niche as a policeman.

Gary grew up in Hopeville and taught for a number of years at the Meadowbrook Elementary School, before leaving to take a principal position in Boston. Now, eleven years later, the native son had returned. As the newly appointed principal of his old school, Meadowbrook, he was anxious to introduce himself to Chief Velone and get to know him better.

When the Chief greeted Gary in the lobby he graciously ushered him into his private conference room, a spacious, airy place with soft yellow walls and a large mahogany table surrounded by comfortable-looking dark brown leather chairs. The chief was a striking man and

Gary was instantly impressed with his meticulous physical appearance, especially his neatly groomed white hair and pressed uniform that gave him a noticeable professional bearing that was obviously a result of his many years spent as a state trooper.

"Good to meet you, Chief."

"Good to meet you," Velone said as he gave Gary a hearty smile. "I've heard good things about you. We're really glad to have you back in town."

"Good to be back, Chief. I've heard good things about you too. We are fortunate to have you as the new chief. You will like the folks here in Hopeville."

After saying enough unctuous things to one another and talking about police work and the state of education in Hopeville, Gary turned to a hot topic. "I understand that Norman Stedman has been charged with the murder of five-year-old Justin Doherty after he confessed to killing the boy."

Velone hesitated before responding. "Yes, that's right. I'm sure you have read the newspaper accounts of the crime. It's been a chilling and brutal case. It's saddened this town like nothing else in its history. No one thought so horrible a thing could occur here in this quiet little town. It's sickened many people, including myself."

"Sometimes there are no answers to why such things happen," Gary said. "When I read that Norman had confessed, I was totally shocked. I knew his dad many years ago and met with him several times after his wife, Norman's mother, died. I had Norman as a student in my fourth grade class at Meadowbrook. I think he was nine years old when his mother died."

Velone was curious. "Why were you shocked?"

"Well, I remember Norman as a curly-haired, chubby kid with big owl-like glasses. He was different in some ways, but seemed happy and content. He got along with other kids in my class by making them laugh with the funny stories he wrote. He had a very active imagination. He also did well academically. I must admit that I found him delightful, although a bit off beat and distant. He had real difficulty in making close friends, although I felt he was making some progress in that area until his mother died suddenly. I can't believe that the little boy I knew turned into a child killer. I just can't believe it!"

"You mentioned that things changed after his mother died?" Velone asked.

"Yes, I had to talk with his dad because Norman had gotten depressed and his school work suffered as a result. He obviously loved his mother greatly and missed her dearly."

Measuring his words carefully, Velone said, "Norman is a very sick guy. I can't believe that the state psychologists found him sane. He needs to be institutionalized and given long term professional help. It's unlikely that he will ever be able to be released from prison."

Velone paused, and then asked, "Why are you so interested in Norman other than trying to understand why one of your past students turned into a child killer?"

Gary hesitated, trying to gather his thoughts. "There are a couple of reasons, I guess. First, I have an interest as a school principal in keeping children out of harm's way. As a school administrator, I have seen a frightening increase in sexual and physical abuse of young children. I strongly feel that educators and law enforcement people have to do a better job of informing parents and children about taking the necessary precautions and better tracking and reporting sexual predators.

"I agree in principle," Velone said. "However, some things are beyond parents' control. Bizarre things just happen and it is not due to the lack of vigilance by parents. It's not their fault."

"Do you feel that was the case in the murder of Justin?" Gary asked.

"Most definitely," Velone said. "Who would think that Norman Stedman was a violent sociopath at age sixteen and would end up killing an innocent little boy?"

His last comment led to the second reason for Gary's interest in Justin's murder case. "That's what baffles me, Chief. What made Norman go over the edge and why didn't anyone see it? I realize I was out of town at the time, but why didn't the police realize that Norman was a troubled young man who really needed to be checked out? He wasn't even brought in for questioning."

"I can't answer that question, Gary, I wasn't here. But, it's a question I often ask myself."

Gary wasn't satisfied with Velone's response. "Someday when I have a lot of time I plan to thoroughly research this case and try to find some answers. How could the Norman Stedman I knew as a happy, pleasant boy at age nine turn into a child killer a few years later?"

"It happens," Velone said, "and sometimes nothing will stop it."

Gary didn't fully agree. "I realize the death of his mother was devastating to him but why didn't anyone try to help him? This was a kid who needed intense counseling especially during his adolescence, but didn't get it. Then again, many children lose a mother early in their life but don't end up like Norman. What drove him to murder? How sad all this is, especially for the poor Doherty family."

Chapter 41

The years flew by. After twenty years as the Meadowbrook Elementary School principal and forty years as a public school educator, Gary Thomas was retiring.

His wife had passed away five years earlier and his three grown children had moved out of town. He was in decent health and had time on his hands. He sat lazily by his kitchen window and looked at the dirty white snow that had accumulated on his back porch from a surprise storm the week before. The temperature had been so cold in recent days that the crusty mounds of snow that had formed resembled a miniature model of a small mountain chain in the Rockies.

Gary thought, "What do I do today?" This is a question that newly retired people ask themselves daily, unless they have found some reason to get out of bed in the morning. Gary wasn't fully at that point yet, but getting there. His options were more like, "Do I continue my hermit existence and read novels all day or do I feed those strange-looking blackbirds tip-toeing on the slippery snow in my backyard?"

Living alone can be boring for some people, especially for someone like Gary who spent years confronting the high verbal demands and unrelenting pace of a school principal's job. This is not to say he didn't have a daily routine around his house. He did, and today was no exception.

He went out his kitchen door to retrieve the local morning newspaper at 7 a.m., as he did every day, tiptoeing like the blackbirds over the ice in the driveway.

Returning inside, he made himself a cup of steaming decaffeinated tea, plopped down in his soft leather recliner and glanced at the picture on the front page of the newspaper. It showed Velone receiving an award from the local Rotary Club. Except for a few minor facial wrinkles, the Chief looked as handsome and impressive as ever.

It was then that it hit him. He remembered his discussion with the

Velone years before about his desire to thoroughly research the Justin Doherty case in order to find answers to some unanswered questions and to separate fact from fiction as best he could. His strong feelings about the case hadn't changed. He now had the time to delve deeply into the crime. Why not? Maybe he might even accomplish some good and jar himself out of his current "retirement jet lag."

Except for the petition drives initiated by Jane Doherty to keep Norman in jail when he requested parole in 1992 and 1997, the case seemed pretty well forgotten. He seriously felt some things should never be forgotten, especially if they deliver a poignant message to parents and children.

Norman Stedman was now forty eight-years-old and had been in prison for twenty-five years and it was just a matter of time before he might be walking the streets again. Hopeville residents, past and present, should remember what happened in May 1975, and almost happened again in April 1982. The case surely has more relevance in today's society than it did over thirty years ago.

Gary wondered how he would approach his long-delayed research and quest for the truth. It was time to call Velone and get his opinion.

When he talked to the Chief, he found him most encouraging and even offered his assistance. "Send me a signed personal letter requesting to review our police file of the case. You have every right to review the case under the Freedom of Information Act.

"Although you probably already know most of the people you should interview, I would gladly suggest some names that might not be on your list. Unfortunately, some key people are no longer around and have died or retired."

Gary good-naturedly took exception to the Chief's last comment, "Are you saying if you're retired, you're dead?"

The Chief laughed, "No, I didn't mean it that way. Hey, I'm at retirement age and hopefully I'll be alive and healthy when I finally do retire."

After their phone conversation, Gary got excited. His mind was racing with ideas about how to find answers to the unanswered questions about the crime, especially confronting the series of rumors that have persisted over the years. He was anxious to start his research and looked forward to hopefully unveiling the truth about Justin's murder.

He knew he had to do one thing right away and that was to arrange to visit or at least call or write Norman in prison and ask him some important questions. Norman's father had died in 1990 and no one seemed to know if Norman had any next of kin who might be visiting him in prison.

Unfortunately, the chances of his talking to close family members about what went on inside the Stedman household weren't good. Even if there were relatives, it was unlikely that they would talk to him and share their painful memories, but he needed to find out. Their information would be helpful when he delved into the sociological and psychological factors that drove Norman to commit such an unspeakable crime.

However, Gary accepted the fact that he might not uncover all the details about what made Norman become violent. There were sure to be information gaps and all he could do was speculate. But still, he was optimistic that if he dug deep enough getting additional information and insight about the crime was possible. He also realized that he most likely would have to promise those who talked to him anonymity along with changing the crime setting to another state or else no one would talk to him.

Jane Doherty had died in 2000. He knew the Doherty family, but had very little contact with them while Meadowbrook principal since the Doherty children had already moved on to other schools and Jane had resigned from her job as a school crossing guard after the arrest of Norman. He had to rely on remaining family members, friends, classmates, neighbors, and key policemen such as Thurston, Harrison, and Velone to share their perceptions about this tragedy, particularly the immediate and long range effect it may have had on its victims.

In spite of these limitations to his research, Gary was anxious to begin and hoped to uncover some answers.

Chapter 42

The first step Gary took was to arrange to talk with Norman. However, when he tried to communicate directly with him, wherever he was incarcerated, to ask him a series of key questions, he found himself stonewalled by state corrections officials at every turn. He couldn't understand why the officials wouldn't at least let him call or send Norman a letter through their office, or even allow him a prison visit if Norman agreed to put him on his visitor list. What was the big deal? Why all these stumbling blocks?

On the advice of Velone, Gary decided to call the chief legal counsel in the Department of Corrections, Kathy Cunningham, and get her take on why he was being denied access to Norman. After a few days, she returned his call.

"Kathy, can you explain to me why I can't somehow communicate with Norman. I don't have to know where he is incarcerated. All I want to do is see if he would be willing to answer a few questions."

She quickly responded, "The major problem we have is one of liability. If something should happen to Norman in prison, both our office and the out-of-state prison are liable and subject to litigation."

"Even if I send a confidential letter to your office and you forwarded it to Norman for me?"

"There is no such thing as a confidential letter to a prisoner," she snapped, making me feel a bit stupid.

"All letters are read by us and the out-of-state correction officers where Stedman is currently incarcerated. We run a huge liability risk with such letters because some prison official could read the letter and inadvertently leak information exposing Stedman as a child killer to the general inmate population; if that happened, he would be dead meat in a very short time."

"You implied he might be in the general inmate population. Wouldn't he be in a prison hospital?"

"No, not necessarily. Because he is in tight protective security, I would suspect he is part of the general inmate population where he is also getting psychological support."

"Your office gave me his inmate identification number, but I wonder if he has any next of kin listed on his profile."

"Let me check our data base." After a few seconds she said, "I have his profile on my screen but I don't see any next of kin listed."

Gary asked, "I wonder if he has any visitors or has an approved call list? "

"I doubt he has any visitors, but only the prison where he is currently would know that. You see Stedman has to abide by their policies in those matters and so do we. We have no control over all that. But you should know that all visitations and telephone calls are also monitored with hard line criminals like Stedman."

Gary was getting frustrated by her clipped bureaucratic and put down responses. "Do I have to initiate legal action to see him?"

"You could but it would be fruitless and a waste of money. I'm sorry I can't be of more help to you," she said.

"So am I," Gary said as he hung up.

Gary decided to call a criminal lawyer friend, Burton Zinn, and get his opinion on the stonewalling he had experienced from the Department of Corrections. He and Burton were roommates and drinking buddies when he lived and taught in Boston while Burton was getting his law degree at Harvard. An extremely bright and capable defense lawyer, Burton was highly respected and successful, having won several high profile cases in recent years.

Burton commiserated with Gary and told him he would be glad to petition the court, but doubted they would allow him to contact Norman in any form. Gary asked him what happens when Norman walks out of jail a free man, whenever that might be. He said his understanding was that Norman was not subject to the sexual predator laws since he was convicted prior to their passage in the 1990's.

"So that means the victims, neighbors, and police will not be notified when Norman is released from prison," Gary asked.

"That's right. He will not be classified as a Level III sexual offender, which he would have been under the current law. The police chief would obviously know about his release, but victims and neighbors would not receive written notification, as is the case now. But remember one thing. Stedman was sentenced to fifty years with ten of those years suspended. That means he will be under the supervision of the state probation division for ten years and will have to report to their office and be subject to their supervision."

"Sorry, Burton, that doesn't give me much comfort. Most people in Hopeville wanted him put away for good and not have him walking the streets again. Velone said that if Norman does walk on or before or even after 2023, he would quickly petition to have the court publicly release the infamous sealed journal. Being one of the few people who have actually read the journal, he feels strongly that Norman should be institutionalized under psychiatric care for the remainder of his life. He clearly feels he can't be cured or rehabilitated. He also said if the court refused to release the journal he would take action to have existing sexual predator laws amended to cover high profile parolees like Norman who have committed heinous capital crimes prior to the passage of the current law.

"Finally, when and if Norman is released, Velone would notify other police chiefs and town officials in the community or communities where Norman lives and works and explain to them Norman's past criminal history. Believe me, the Chief got really worked up when I asked him about the possibility of Norman getting early probation or eventually being allowed to reenter society."

"Whatever he wants to do, that's Velone's prerogative," Burton said. "I sometimes wonder if plea bargains cause more problems than they solve. In order to avoid a grim and grisly trial for the victims by reducing Stedman's charge from first to second degree murder, an excellent chance for putting Stedman away for life without parole was lost. Now, the victims have to deal with sensational parole hearings and with Stedman walking away a free man on or before the completion of his sentence in 2023. The case never goes away."

Burton then started to lecture Gary. "Our judicial system is not perfect. Remember, the judge, Velone and the lawyers involved read the horrible details that Stedman wrote in his journal, you didn't. You don't want the victims or their children or grandchildren to read what Stedman did to that young child. Also, for every parolee who is released from jail and returns to society a very small percentage kill again. Unfortunately, when they do kill again it is glamorized and sensationalized by the media and the public doesn't understand that it is one in a thousand or more case situation."

Gary looked bothered. "Burton, even given your statistics, I find it difficult to believe that it's that rare of an occurrence. And anyway, even if it's a one in one thousand case I care about the one, don't you?"

Chapter 43

As Gary continued his research on Norman, he decided to talk to numerous people who could give him greater insight into this complex man and help him better understand why he turned into a barbaric killer at such an early age. His teachers, fellow actors, neighbors, high school and college classmates, relatives, the police and, of course, the Dohertys and Richmonds were on his interview list. Hopefully, they could shed some light on Norman and his anti-social personality.

Unfortunately, depending upon the long-term memory of people doesn't always result in getting reliable information. Although the general population in Hopeville may have forgotten the Justin Doherty case, most of the people Gary planned to interview either had direct involvement in the case or had personal interactions with Norman. They also had amazing recall. It is similar to the type of recall people have when you ask them about Pearl Harbor, President Kennedy's assassination, or September 11, 2001.

Of course, there were exceptions. For example, one old codger who participated in the search told Gary, "Young fellow, you are asking me about something that happened over thirty years ago. God, I can't remember what I had for breakfast this morning."

One of the first people Gary talked with was Detective Chuck Harrison. Now in his early sixties, he had recently retired as a criminal investigator after forty years, most of them as a homicide detective. Although he now lived in New Jersey, Gary was fortunate to meet up with him during his annual pilgrimage to Hopeville, a time when he visits relatives and goes fishing with old buddies.

As they sat in Gary's den, Chuck looked more like a man in his late forties with his ruddy complexion and a full head of light brown hair yet to turn gray, a man too young to be thinking about collecting Social Security checks.

As they reviewed the Doherty case, Chuck said something that struck Gary. It was in response to one of Gary's many questions, "Do you think Norman was a potential serial killer, possibly a future mass murderer?"

Chuck had a ready answer. "Even though he wasn't technically one at the time, in my opinion he was on his way to becoming one. We don't know what would have happened if he had killed Donnie Richmond and got away with it."

"Although somewhat speculative, that is an interesting point," Gary said.

"You say speculative? Maybe, maybe not. He went from killing a five-year-old to attempting to kill a fourteen-year- old. It's a progressive Peeping Tom sort of thing. First, the serial killer looks in a window. Then he climbs in the window. And finally he sexually assaults and kills the innocent victim."

"Do you think he killed anyone else between his murdering of Justin in 1975 and his attempted murder of Donnie Richmond in 1982?"

"Not that we know of. Anything that came in relating to young kids or teenagers we paid close attention to, knowing that the Justin Doherty case was still an open case."

"Do you think if Norman had been more independent and not restricted by living at home, he might have had greater opportunity to kill and most likely would have killed other people from 1975 to 1982?"

"It's very possible," Chuck said. "He lived with his dad, his stepmother, and his grandmother in the same small house. He didn't drive or have a car. He either walked or hitchhiked everywhere. It wasn't until 1980 when both his grandmother and stepmother had died that he could be alone in his home for long stretches of time. Of course, he also was not someone we were ever suspicious about either. He wasn't on our radar screen mainly because his father was a reserve policeman and quite active in that group."

During the next few days, Harrison's comments made Gary think about the profiles of serial killers and theories about what factors cause a sociopath to commit criminal violence. He remembered reading articles about how current research refutes the notion that violence is solely caused by biological factors. It is not just a matter of a change in testosterone levels or a change in brain activity. It is not solely a matter of impulsivity, aggression, and violence being in the genes.

After his conversation with Harrison, Gary wanted to know more about sociopath behavior so he contacted an old college buddy of his, Harold Godfrey, who was a neuroscientist in Boston.

After explaining his intended research, he asked his friend, "Aren't the roots of violence more complicated than simply saying a killer like Norman was just 'wired at birth'?"

Harold paused, thinking how to answer so Gary could best understand. "Current theory suggests that criminal violence is caused by an accumulation of factors, sociological as well as biological. The biological factors are meaningless outside the context of the social factors and environment in which it occurs. It is the innate traits and experiences of Norman Stedman as he interacts with his environment that most likely caused him to become a killer."

That raised an interesting question in Gary's mind. If Norman had grown up in a different environment would he have progressed from being a lonely, isolated boy to a child killer? Again, maybe, maybe not.

As a young child Norman loved *Dark Shadows*, the popular television series from the 1970's that enjoys cult status among its intense followers. He especially loved the vampire in the show, Barnabas Collins. Obviously, something in Norman's biological makeup attracted him to the dark side of life and he saw Barnabas as his hero.

But not all young boys who loved Barnabas turned into bloody murderers. Nor do all young boys who have anti-social personalities and live in their own bleak little worlds become violent adults. Although Norman's biology may have played a key role, the product of his experiences interacting with that biology may have been the reason he became a child killer.

This theory explains why mass murderers may have different profiles. Some are highly social, glib, even charming con artists like John Wayne Gacy and Ted Bundy. Some are shy and withdrawn like Jeffrey Dahmer. Differences in personalities can be attributed to differences in the environments they lived in as well as their different genetic make-ups. Forensic psychologists have attempted to identify common characteristics among serial killers, and when looking at their list it is interesting to see how those commonalities fit Norman.

Gary conducted an Internet search and reviewed the writings of noted criminologists Eric Hickey, Robert Ressler, Ann Burgess, and Robert Keppel. Their data bases confirmed the fact that there are several typologies of serial killers. Serial killers also go through several stages and share similar characteristics depending upon their typology. Their data reveals that mass murderers tend to be white males, usually between twenty-five and thirty-five, and can be classified as "organized or disorganized" depending upon the type of evidence recovered at the crime scene. More are psychotic than organized killers. Some use alcohol or drugs to dominate and kill their victims. Most experience considerable family dysfunction. Some give obvious warnings like violence-filled writings, others strike unexpectedly, kill people they know, target any one handy, and are socially isolated. They tend to blame everyone for their problems but themselves. They seem to be aggrieved and hurt. They are usually educated and intelligent and without conscience.

Burgess explains that some mass murderers are angry and want to take it out on the world. She talks of a category of killer "who has a fantasy life as a child where he has complete control, while the other phase is the shell that walks thorough the real world with little energy and effort committed to being emotionally isolated with his own fantasies." Gary thought this might be the case with Norman. He appeared to want power and control over a world that left him powerless.

Gary hoped that through his extensive interviews he could determine if Norman had experienced a prolonged series of frustrations caused by rejection, insults, and indifference from those around him. Did he seek power, control and fame, but unfortunately was unable to form genuine, sustaining, and lasting relationships?

It was time to schedule his interviews and get some answers. With Velone's additions, he had over sixty people on his list.

Chapter 44

Gary realized that Norman's experiences in Hopeville as a child and as a young man most likely contributed to the emergence of his anti-social personality and eventual transformation into a killer. He was interested to learn whether factors like Norman's social unease, aloofness, and physical appearance may have played a large role in that transformation.

His hope was to gain greater insight into those and other factors that may have contributed to his aberrant behavior. What were his relationships with those relatives he lived with really like? What would his former teachers, classmates, and fellow actors say about him? How about his neighbors and their children? What impressions and memories do they have of Norman as a small boy, teenager, and young adult?

Gary had other questions. Did his peers taunt him? Did he have any close friends? How did he handle rejection? Did they see him express any emotion such as pent up anger or fury? Or joy or enthusiasm? Did he have a sense of humor? Was he bright and a talented actor, singer, and writer? Did he ever have a serious, personal conversation with someone where he revealed some of his bare feelings? Were you shocked when you learned he had murdered Justin?

Prior to conducting his personal interviews, Gary decided to review old newspaper articles and how they described Norman. He even went to the town library and found what Norman had written in the class will when a senior in high school:

"I, Norman Stedman, do hereby bequest my tremendous talent (who am I kidding) to the Drama Club. I also leave them my hope for much luck and success."

His words sounded like those of any normal high school student. However, under his yearbook picture he wrote a more revealing line: "*I may look like I am moving slow, but I am going faster than you think.*"

Reporters from local and state newspapers had interviewed some of Norman's classmates and neighbors. Generally they all said the same thing—Norman was a loner. He tried to be a part of things but didn't really know how to go about it. His life centered on the theatre in both high school and college. Although he was comfortable in his participation with the Community Players, there was a distance between him and other actors. He had few, if any, close friends at school or with the Players and was at times tolerated because of his hard work and dedication to their theatrical productions.

One paper reported that, "Outside his circle of fellow drama students, he was shunned by many and even ridiculed and taunted by classmates because of his weight and appearance. His teachers felt pity for him at seeing how he was treated." Gary definitely wanted to check the validity of that statement while interviewing those on his interview list.

After his arrest, the newspapers also had a few sketchy comments from Norman's neighbors such as, "He was always very, very polite. I couldn't say a bad word about him" and "I thought he would grow up and become a famous actor or director."

It was reported that a distant cousin said, "He never gave his father any trouble. All he wanted was friends and some good conversation."

These comments lacked sufficient detail. Gary wanted to know more about specific interactions people had with Norman and what influenced their impressions of him. After interviewing sixty different people, a clearer picture emerged.

Chapter 45

The feedback Gary gathered from interviews with Norman's high school classmates, teachers, and administrators was most revealing.

One young lady in his high school drama club said:
"When I heard Norman confessed to murder, I lost it and almost passed out. In drama club, he liked to play the dark character roles. He thought he was a talented actor, but really wasn't. He was slovenly and unkempt and his pants were usually dragging on the floor—the in-thing now, but of course wasn't the style in the 1970's. He was not picked on in the drama club, because of the type of kids attracted to that type of activity, but was mocked by others in school who would say things to him like, 'Hey, Tuba, move it!'"

Another young lady in his drama club had this to say:
"Norman lacked self-confidence and didn't trust anyone. He wanted to be alone and sat by himself at lunch. One time, I asked him to join me and some of my friends at our lunch table. He actually got angry and very defensive saying, 'You don't want me there. All you are doing is making yourself feel good.' He never really had any friends, but then again didn't appear to want any.

"Norman impressed me as someone not well taken care of—I mean that more than just his unkempt physical appearance. You wonder about what went on in his home life and how it might have affected his personality. At seventeen in the 1970's, there were a lot of weird kids in our school, but Norman definitely stood out. Then again, he seemed to be content being that way."

A young man who appeared in a variety show with Norman shared his observations:
"He was a quiet kid. I saw him as expressionless. No outward signs

of anger or any other emotion for that matter. No laughter, hostility, excitement, nothing. Although he was very different, he appeared content to be in his own skin. He may have had real repressed anger, but as I said, he appeared contented. In his junior year, I remember Norman participating in a skit in our annual spring variety show. The skit was a take-off on the old Life cereal commercial with the chant, 'Give it to Normie, he will eat anything.' Given the rumors of what he did with the young boy's dead body, it is horrible for me to recall that scene now. You wonder if he had a moral conscience."

Another male classmate provided this insight:
"I sat behind Norman in a couple of classes. He never said much in class. He was very twitchy and nervous. He always wore black clothes, especially a long black woolen trench coat, you know, like those Navy trench coats. Although he might have been clean-shaven in his yearbook picture, most of the time he had a goatee and sideburns that were never trimmed and just grew haphazardly down his face. He was so strange and eccentric that I was not surprised when I heard he murdered the Doherty boy, because he fit the description of someone who might do such a horrible thing. He wore the same clothes all the time, appeared like he didn't bathe much and seemed to have dirty, oily hair."

His high school principal made this interesting comment:
"He was physically unusual with a funny body shape—a large, overweight fellow who looked dumpy and soft with a big posterior. He lumbered around school hugging one side of the corridor carrying his book bag. I never saw him with anybody. He seemed like a serious and sensitive young man with a keen interest in theatre and was a good dutiful student. He was not someone whose parents I needed to contact and recommend psychological counseling or referral to a psychiatrist. I did have a few students over the years that needed that type of help, but Norman wasn't one of them."

A former history teacher and football coach who like many people observed Norman from a distance said:
"I never had Norman in class. Never knew him. I was shocked when I learned he was one of our past students and was arrested for

murder. But then again, I was told that Norman was like a shadow in school, almost invisible. It is not surprising I did not know him."

His drama coach and English teacher had this impression:
"I was drama coach and directed Norman in a medieval play we presented. I was shocked when I heard he had been arrested for murder. I also had him in English class and although very nervous and lacking in self-confidence, he was a good, conscientious student. He never displayed any irrational behavior that would lead one to think he needed counseling. I also never saw him picked on in class nor would I allow that to happen. He was always taping his glasses together to the point that I contacted the Lion's Club to see if they could provide new glasses for him. The one word I would use to describe the Norman I knew would be 'nervous' as he constantly wiped his sweaty hands on his pants."

The new principal's observation was limited and a bit different:
"I came to the high school during Norman's senior year. I had little contact with him. He did however physically remind me of King Tut, the villain in the Batman television series."

One of his drama teachers talked of Norman's dedication to acting:
"I worked with the Drama Club on several plays and remember Norman playing certain roles in our productions. He was average as an actor but he always learned his lines, was extremely dedicated to our club, and was most reliable. Although he kept to himself, his hard work got him elected as club president and he won an acting award."

A high school teacher who tried to befriend Norman but found it difficult to reach him had this to say:
"Norman was in several of my classes over his four years in high school. He was a decent student. He was a lonely kid and I tried to befriend him, to reach out to him because he was a bit of a sad soul. He would drop into my classroom after class a few days each week. I sensed he was never in a rush to go home. We talked about numerous things, but it was usually about school and his drama activities. The conversations were shallow, just friendly chatter and some bantering on both sides. He seemed to be hungry for conversation with an adult.

I guess he had a certain trust in me and knew I wouldn't probe into personal matters. My classroom was like a safe haven for him. One time, when he was a senior I gave him a ride home. He asked me to drop him off in downtown Hopeville. I told him I would take him to his house, although I didn't know where it was at the time. When I learned later that he lived on Suffork Street across from Justin Doherty's house, I wondered if he just didn't want me to know that."

A classmate who attended college with Norman shared this observation:

"After high school, I ran into Norman again when he was hanging around the Fine Arts Building in his sophomore year in college. He was wearing a long black drooping trench coat and a type of wide brim black painter's hat with one side tilted like a famous actor might wear to announce his presence to the world."

A fellow actor in the Community Players with Norman put it succinctly and may have been right on target:

"He wasn't stupid but because of his physical anomalies, he looked that way. As an actor he could escape from the person who he was and didn't like and be someone else in the theatre."

Chapter 46

Neighbors knew little about what went on inside the Stedman house. The Stedmans were a private family and unlike the rest of the neighbors had little interaction with other families on Suffork Street. The window shades were always pulled down and very few people ever set foot inside their house.

Gary did however manage to track down a former neighborhood playmate of Norman's by the name of Billy Alfred who was actually in the Stedman house on a couple of occasions. Billy was managing a bar in Houston, Texas, and it was difficult for Gary to hear him on the phone over background noise from bar patrons who appeared to be singing some off-color songs.

"How did you get in the house?" Gary yelled into the telephone receiver.

"Norman wanted me to see something he thought I might be interested in."

"Before we get to that, what was the house like?" Gary asked.

Billy hesitated before he spoke, "Well, it was a pigsty—the biggest mess you can imagine. And it smelled bad. I remember two ladies volunteered to clean the house one time before Fred got married again."

Gary was curious, "What did Norman want to show you?"

"It was about 1979 and while we were sitting in his living room, he told me about a play he was in and showed me a skull that he said was a prop he was using. When he confessed to the murder and the police recovered a skull, I wondered if the skull he showed me was Justin's. To this day, the thought of that scene in the living room sticks like glue in my mind."

"Did other kids in the neighborhood pick on him?" Gary asked.

"Most of the kids avoided him, because they thought he was a weirdo. Some said he was gay, but I don't know; that impression however was reinforced because he was always sitting on the curb in front of his house staring at kids playing across the street. He rarely played with us. The only time I can remember Norman joining us was once he played some basketball with me and a few other kids; otherwise, he stayed to himself. But I always thought that he was pretty smart."

"What about his Dad?"

"I didn't know his Dad that well. He wasn't home much, but was friendly enough always giving me a wave when he was in his car. He and his wife appeared to spend most of their time together sitting in their cars in their driveway reading."

Gary had another question. "When you learned that Norman confessed to the killing, what did you think?"

"I was shocked because Norman was so young. Who'd think he'd do something like that at age sixteen?"

After talking to Billy, Gary placed a call to Wally Sherry in San Jose, California. Wally was a playmate of Norman's when he first moved into the neighborhood at age nine. After a series of calls, Gary tracked Wally down at a restaurant in downtown San Jose. It was a noisy, but interesting call.

After exchanging greetings, Gary explained the purpose of his call and Wally readily agreed to answer his questions.

"Tell me about those days when you played with Norman. What was he like?" Gary asked.

"Well, he tried to get a number of kids to play with him, but most chose not to. Their parents might have had something to do with that, I don't know. I was an exception, because to me he was a bit intriguing, a different sort of kid. He loved to run around the yard playing that Dark Shadows guy or other weird characters. He also liked to cut up toads and frogs. So, I was one of the few who played with him."

Gary was again curious. "What was he like at that age? I am interested in how you would describe his personality."

"Oh, he was very insecure and sensitive. It bothered him that most of the kids wouldn't play with him. When a few did play with him, he tried to befriend them. He desperately wanted them to come back. He wanted to bond with us kids, but never could. I remember that after playing with him, he would give me and other kids' gifts. I'm talking about expensive gifts! One time, he gave me a first class camera and I took it home and my mother asked me where I got it. When I told her she told me to return it immediately."

"What was your reaction when you heard he had killed Justin?"

"Like most people I was shocked. He seemed to be a passive, harmless, pathetic guy. But when you put all the pieces together, you can understand why he turned into a violent killer. We all live lives of quiet desperation, but who would think that Norman was that sick inside?"

Wally's opinion dovetailed somewhat with Gary's. Wally was quite perceptive. He said when you put all the pieces together you could understand why Norman murdered Justin. This was not the case for Gary; he still needed to learn more about those pieces, and how they came together causing Norman to turn into a violent killer.

Gary next wanted to talk with some of the adult neighbors who had lived on Suffork Street from at least 1975 through 1982. Unfortunately, only three families still lived there. The rest had either relocated or died. However, Gary was able to contact some former neighbors who now lived out of state or elsewhere in the Hopeville area. He decided to begin his interviews with the Jenks family who lived next door to the house where the Stedmans had lived.

Todd and Mabel Jenks have lived in the same house on Suffork Street for forty years. Todd was the fireman that checked the Stedman cellar with Norman close at his side during the search. Mabel also knew Jane Doherty having served with her as a school crossing guard.

Sitting at their kitchen table, the couple openly responded to Gary's questions.

"Mabel, how well did you know the Stedmans?"

"Really not that well. They pretty much kept to themselves. Oh, we did talk to Fred occasionally when we met in the yard. He was very cordial, but different, just like Norman."

"Todd, tell me about your conversations with Fred."

"It was just normal neighbor stuff, gardening, local issues, weather, that sort of thing," Many times, Norman was with Fred, standing in back of him. He didn't get engaged in any conversation whatsoever. Fred did all of the talking."

Mabel added, "Yes, and every time Norman tried to talk to us, his grandmother would call him and tell him to get back in the house. It was almost like she didn't want him to talk to us."

Gary asked, "In all the years you lived next door did you ever go inside their house?"

"We never did," Mabel said. "We were in every other house on the street at one time or another, but never in the Stedman house."

"Do you have any other insights about the Stedmans you would care to share?"

"From time to time, you could hear Norman's stepmother in heated arguments with Norman," Mabel said. "A lot of the disagreement related to his reluctance to attend to his personal hygiene. Poor Fred, he was a passive guy but must have had his hands full in keeping peace in his home."

"Do you mean that Norman was like Howard Hughes, who in later stages of his life just let his physical appearance go, not shaving, not taking baths, not cleaning or changing his clothes, that sort of thing?"

"Exactly. Intelligent guy too," Mabel said. "It makes you think that this seems to be a problem when people have mental problems. It's like a signal that something is seriously wrong with a person."

"One other thing I observed bothered me," Mabel continued. "Fred got a new truck one time. I can recall how he and his wife had Norman sit in the back of the truck when they went downtown. I know it is no big thing, but when it is frigid weather and you see large-sized Norman sitting in the open exposed to the elements, it makes you wonder about the type of relationship he had with the adults in his house. I actually felt sorry for the poor kid every time I saw him."

Gary asked Todd if he had ever noticed anything else about the family that could shed some light on what they were like.

"Not too much. But there were a couple of odd things that happened with some of the animals they had."

"Odd in what way?" Gary asked.

"Well, one time the animal control office was called in because Norman's black cat went crazy. It flew around out of control, bouncing off the walls and even attacked Norman. You wonder why it suddenly became deranged. They finally had to corner the cat in Norman's bedroom and take it away."

"What about the other odd thing?"

"The second incident was very strange. Either Norman or Fred had a dog one time and left it tied up in the back yard all the time. I mean all the time! The dog was sick and his intestines were actually coming out of his rectum. He also was suffering from malnutrition. It was just awful and something had to be done. We called the ASCPA and they sent a person to Fred's house to check out the situation. The guy said that he had never seen such cruelty to an animal. I was surprised that Norman and Fred weren't arrested for extreme animal neglect."

Gary had a question for Mabel. "Don't you have a son about the same age of Donnie Richmond?"

"Yes we do, his name is Keith."

"Did Norman try to get Keith to drink with him?"

"No, Keith stayed away from Norman. He thought he was weird. When we heard Norman was inviting young boys to his house to drink, we told Keith to never even think about doing it."

Gary asked, "If you knew Norman was giving alcohol to minors why didn't you bring it to the attention of Fred and his wife?"

"Well, Fred's wife was sick for a long time. Neighbors did not want to give him other problems since he had enough to handle as it was. We didn't want to bother them."

Mabel had one more thing to tell Gary, something that got his attention.

"Before you leave, I want you to know that in my heart, I feel that Fred knew what Norman did."

"But he appeared to be really upset when he heard Norman confessed to the killing," Gary said.

"I know but his upset had to do with what was going to happen to his son. Fred had been a policeman; he knew what the consequences were when a person was convicted of murder. He wasn't that limited that he couldn't put 'two and two' together. What do you think those long talks in the car between Fred and Norman were about?"

Gary then interviewed Gloria Richmond, the mother of Donnie, who lived down the street from the Dohertys, Jenks, and Stedmans. She revealed to him a telling incident involving her daughter and Norman.

"My daughter was in a play with Norman put on by the Community

Players. Norman spent a lot of time at the library where the Players used a small auditorium and stage to present their productions."

"Yes, I know he was active with the Players," Gary said. "I have been told that the theatre was his passion and probably his only real outlet."

"Well, one day my daughter went early to the library and went backstage and suddenly spotted Norman sitting in a rocking chair all by himself staring at her. He had a noose around his neck. He looked earnestly at her, but didn't crack a smile. My daughter really thought he was crazy. When my daughter came home that day she was shaken, thinking that Norman had been sitting there contemplating hanging himself. I told her that he probably was just kidding around and trying to shock her."

Chapter 47

To find out more about what made Norman tick, Gary tried to locate people who reached out to him, people who had extended conversations with him, and people that he apparently liked. It was unlikely that he trusted anyone, but maybe he had opened up with someone and shared some of his disappointments and his dreams.

Unfortunately, not many people wanted to revisit the past and talk about Norman Stedman; they wanted to forget him and the dastardly thing he had done to Justin Doherty. Luckily, there were some people that knew him fairly well and were willing to talk to Gary.

Gary was fortunate to find three people who knew that Norman had immense problems and needed help. All three made strong attempts to help him, but with little success. To them, Norman appeared to be in denial. One of them even referred him to the college counseling office twice, but the office could not schedule him because, by policy, Norman had to personally initiate the contact and request counseling.

The first person was Clara Wright, a librarian in Hopeville who was very active in the Community Players as an officer and actress. A small, thin lady in her sixties with piercing brown eyes and straight dark hair, she was a transplant from New York who had attended college in the area, fallen in love with the Berkshires, and eventually stayed and raised her family in Hopeville. Gary asked her about the first time she met Norman.

"It was at the Village Green in the playground area, where I was with a friend. We were watching our young children go down the playground slide, when I saw this heavy guy sitting on a nearby bench. He really looked odd. In fact, I was disquieted by his looks. I turned to my friend and said, 'Who's that guy?' I clearly remember what she said. 'Oh, that's only Norman.' Now, I'm from New York City so I don't expect everyone to look the same, but I tell you this guy looked menacing to me. Later, of course, I found out who he was when I joined the Community Players."

"Did he look disheveled and unkempt?" Gary asked.

"Yes, he dressed that way because he obviously didn't feel good about himself."

Gary asked Clara to describe her relationship with Norman during their time together in the Players.

"We were in several plays together. We had roles in *Jesus Christ Super Star* and Norman directed a play I was in shortly before he was arrested."

"What did the other actors and directors think of him?"

"He worked hard and was very reliable doing all kinds of things as we put on several productions each year. He was particularly good in certain roles. For example, he was in his element when he played Death in *Stop the World I Want to Get Off*. Several of us wondered about him, but we gave him space and tried to make him feel important. I personally went out of my way to make him feel worthwhile."

"What did you wonder about him?" Gary asked.

"Well, he was a strange guy. I remember a discussion I had with one of our directors who taught drama in college and had acted on Broadway. When I suggested that Norman might be gay, this insightful fellow disagreed. He said that he didn't think Norman was an active homosexual, because to be active you need to have contact with other humans.

He felt Norman was not really active socially and didn't have contact with anyone other than fantasy characters in his twisted mind."

Gary was interested in a previous comment made by Clara. "You surprised me when you said that Norman directed you in a play. Tell me about that."

"It was a one act play called, *Lou Gehrig Did Not Die of Cancer*. Norman selected the play and I was cast in one of the roles with two other women. Our group thought it would be a nice gesture to give Norman an opportunity to direct a play particularly since he was thinking about a future career in the theatre."

"How did it go?"

"So, so. When we were rehearsing, Norman and I were at odds. He had all these ideas about acting that he must have picked up from some of his college classes. He really wasn't giving us any real direction and wouldn't listen to some of our suggestions. There were scenes where I just stood around looking like an ornament.

"At one point, I had decided that I was not going on the stage unless some changes were made in the script. The other two ladies in the play were equally upset but were less vocal than I was. They urged me to stick it out. Still not pacified, I went home and rewrote several scenes and decided to do them the way I wanted to in spite of Norman's lack of direction—and on opening night that's exactly what I did."

"The play must have flopped," Gary said.

"No, it didn't. It went off quite well. It's something that he said one night when I was driving him home after a performance that has bothered me for twenty-five years. It has stuck in my throat all that time. It is something I haven't shared with anyone until now."

"Are you serious? What is it?"

"While we were riding, he asked me how I thought he did as a director. Trying to give him a boost, I complimented him and told him the play was well received by the audience and he should be pleased. But I also was honest with him and said if he wanted to improve as a director he really needed to better understand women. He needed to know how to motivate them and how to empathize with them. I told him he didn't have to like them but for heaven's sake don't ignore them. He seemed to take the criticism well."

"That is the nightmare you have been carrying around with you for years?" Gary asked.

"No, it isn't; there is more. As we stopped in front of his house, he asked me another question that totally floored me. He asked me if I knew who John Wayne Gacy was. I said I did. He was the serial killer out of Chicago. He then asked me what I thought of a person like that. I said a person like that must be extremely tortured and unhappy to inflict such pain on other people. Such a person needed a great deal of help."

Gary remembered the John Wayne Gacy story from some research he had done on serial killers. Reportedly, Gacy killed thirty-three people, all of them men. He buried all but four of them in a crawl space under the floor of his house in Norwood Park Township outside of Chicago. They called him the "Clown Killer" for entertaining children in a clown costume during the many parties he threw for his friends and neighbors. His killing rampage spanned from 1977 to 1980. One book recounted how one of his victims managed to live after Gacy lured him into his car with an offer of drugs, used chloroform to knock him out, and sexually attacked him. Gacy kept the dead bodies close to him until they nearly decomposed. He was a fully formed serial killer who went on his rampage immediately after his wife divorced him in 1976.

After they discussed the Gacy case, Gary said to Clara, "The similarities between what Gacy and Norman did are amazing. Norman committed his atrocious crime shortly before Gacy began his killings. The method Gacy used to lure victims, kill them and desecrate their bodies compares closely to what Norman did with Justin and apparently tried to repeat with Donnie Richmond. Norman seemed to act more impulsively with less need and thirst to kill many people. Was he on his way to becoming a serial killer if he hadn't been caught in 1982? I wouldn't bet against it, would you?"

Clara held up her hand like she was stopping traffic. "This is all very grisly and revealing, Gary, but hold on, I am not through with my story yet. There is more."

"There's more?"

"You won't believe this but a few weeks after my conversation with Norman in March, I couldn't find my ten-year-old son, Mark. I live on the other side of town from Norman, but less than a mile away. It was a beautiful, sunny day in April, the same type of day when Justin disappeared. I walked up and down the streets with neighbors and we couldn't find Mark. I started to panic and at that very moment I remembered my conversation with Norman. I made the connection at that point and suddenly felt sick to my stomach.

"When I finally found Mark and we were walking home together I told him that if Norman Stedman ever comes to the door and says something has happened to me and he wants to come in and talk to you, don't let him in. Run immediately out the back door."

"So, Clara, you made this connection between Norman and Justin and didn't know what to do with this revelation, is that what you're saying?"

"Exactly. For twenty-five years I didn't say anything about this to anyone. What do you do with something like that?"

Trying to relieve some of her guilt, Gary said, "Well, when Norman was arrested, the police did make the connection that he may have had something to do with Justin's disappearance too."

"No, you don't understand, Gary! I made my connection in early April about two weeks before Norman tried to strangle the Richmond boy. Look, he could have killed that child!"

Gary said goodbye to Clara and graciously thanked her for her startling interview—it obviously very stressful for her to revisit the past. As he headed for his car, he hoped however that she had gained some peace of mind now that she had finally unloaded the emotional burden she had carried for so long.

Chapter 48

"Dan, do you remember the first time you saw Norman? What were your reactions?"

Gary was conducting an interview with Dan Fredericks on the speakerphone with a tape recorder at his side. Dan was a former college classmate of Norman's who went on to become a successful actor on stage, screen, and television, having significant roles in well known Broadway plays and television series. He was calling from his Manhattan apartment and was willing to share some of his recollections of Norman.

"The first time I saw Norman was in the summer of 1976 when I took a lady friend to the local Community Players' production. I believe it was three one-act plays, one of which was written by Edward Alan Baker, one of my favorite playwrights. I was starting my junior year in college that September.

"Was the play presented on the stage in back of the town library?" Gary asked.

"Yes, it was. When we were seated I looked up on the stage and noticed a large pile of sticks and leaves in the front of the closed curtain. It was about 7:30 p.m. or so. After the first act finished shortly before 9 p.m., we took a stretch break while staying in our seats. Suddenly, as the second act began, this guy appeared from underneath the pile of leaves and I thought, oh my God that guy was under that pile all that time! What type of person would do something like that?

"The fellow had a speech impediment and everything about him was physically unattractive and strange. He lumbered around the stage and his impediment made him hard to understand. I didn't know if this strange guy was a genius actor who had just adopted this character or what. My lady friend and I talked about him for weeks. I couldn't get him out of my mind. Where did this freaky guy come from?"

"Dan, you mentioned you were starting your junior year in college that September. Did you meet Norman there?"

"Yes. All of a sudden he showed up as a freshman in some of my classes. We found out he was not a genius actor, but was playing himself and he did have a speech impediment and did lumber around."

"But don't a lot of people who are different gravitate toward the theatre. What made Norman so different from the rest of the students?"

"Yes, a lot of people who go into theatre have problems. But Norman was extreme and considered to be a freak. Other students couldn't stand him and didn't want to be around him. Others, myself included, wanted to take him under our wing; however, that was a difficult challenge."

"Why was it difficult?"

"Well, for one thing, one of his problems was that he smelled bad."

"I know that problem keeps coming up as I delve deeper into my research on him. Tell me, what did he smell like?"

Dan described the smell as a very unique one. "It was the kind of the smell you get in the Northeast and in Massachusetts in November when you walk by a pile of putrefied leaves. You know, like organic putrefaction that is really rank like a forgotten, wet, old pile of leaves."

Gary said, "Norman hitchhiked everywhere. Did you give him rides to school? Did you try to talk to him and give him any support?"

"Yes, I picked him up several times during his freshman year. I had difficulty engaging him in conversation. He just sat there looking down and didn't make any eye contact. I did most of the talking and he just grunted or gave one or two word responses. I had a 1975 Volkswagen and every time I gave him a ride, my car smelled like those rotten leaves. I had to leave the windows open the next day and air out the car. I stopped giving him a ride after awhile."

"Other than being together in classes were you in any plays together?"

"Yes, in the fall of Norman's freshman year we presented, *Charley's Aunt*. Norman had a big role in the play and was cast as an old man. He had a lot to do and say. I played one of the leads in the play as well."

"How did he do?"

"It was hard for the director to get him to do what he had to do, but Norman was eager to please and worked very hard. It was so peculiar; he was weirdly effective yet strange as he moved around like a wounded, lumbering bear. Interestingly, that was the only time while in college that he was ever cast in any role in a play."

Gary was intrigued by Dan's evaluation of Norman's acting ability. "Are you saying that cast in a specific character role, he was adequate as an actor?"

"Yes, that is somewhat true; however, as I mentioned before, people didn't want to be around him. He was considered a pariah and an anomaly and this separated him from other students. That sort of impression doesn't endear you to those in the acting profession."

Gary could understand his point, but had more questions. "Dan, what was his relationship like with his professors?"

"It was contentious, not in class, but outside of class in the conversations he had with them about his work and about class. He was always uttering obscenities under his breath after disagreements with them. I heard him call them bastards, bitches and whores. Interestingly, he seemed to have more contentious relationships with female professors than with male professors. Some of his professors felt sorry for him, others wondered what he was doing in the theatre department."

Gary asked him what he thought of Norman's personal appearance.

"Often it seemed like he always wore the same old pair of jeans and the same flannel shirt. He also wore an orange down jacket all the time, even in warm weather. He was a guy I tried to talk to and help as much as I could. But he just wouldn't respond to me or to anyone else for that matter, so I gave up."

Gary then asked Dan a question that he asked everyone he interviewed. "Did Norman experience a great deal of rejection while in college?"

"Yes, he did. Not being cast in plays, not having the scripts he wrote being highly valued, and of course being mocked by other students."

Gary asked Dan to tell me more about the mocking.

"The best illustration I can give you has to do with Norman's auditions for our musical productions. He sang the same song, over and over again, at each audition, as his fellow students snickered. I think the song was *All By Myself* by Eric Carmen. He had a dreadful voice.

A group of theatre students had great fun singing Norman's song by mimicking him and exaggerating his lisp. It was a bit cruel."

After finishing his conversation with Dan, Gary tried to imagine Norman in college interacting with students and professors in the theatre department. He must have been one of the most memorable students they had ever encountered; memorable, that is, in a sad way. Poor Norman was evidently now seen as a freak in an environment that until this point had welcomed him and provided him with a healthy outlet and genuine satisfaction. He now faced failure in the one area where he had previously achieved some acclaim and a positive identity. Now, his long held dreams of becoming a professional actor were being brutally crushed and worst, he was seen as weird by fellow theatre students.

Because of the increasing rejection, Gary wondered if, because of the increasing rejection, Norman was becoming convinced that his professors in their ignorance were ruining his life. All college seemed to provide him was constant frustration. The growing fury and rage inside him was becoming more difficult to hide.

It was time for Gary to contact the theatre professor who knew him best. He wanted to know more about the problems Norman had in his relationships with other students and with those professors he felt were standing in his way of a successful career in the theatre.

Chapter 49

Before interviewing the next person on his list, a college professor who reportedly had a contentious relationship with Norman, Gary ran across an old newspaper article in the Hopeville Times that piqued his interest.

Shortly after his arrest, a newspaper had published excerpts of poetry and prose written by Norman that dealt with death, grieving parents and a young boy taken forever from his home. The excerpts provided Gary with a new avenue to better understand what might have been going on in Norman's distorted mind.

The reporter who wrote the article was a former college classmate of Norman's in a creative writing course he had taken during his freshman year in college. The course assignment called for students, after they had written a poem or narrative, to distribute copies of their articles to all members of the class. By searching his old college files, the reporter remembered Norman and found a poem of his that described a classical mythological character named Ganymede, a beautiful young boy who was carried off to Olympus by the god Zeus to be the cupbearer for the gods.

The poem read:

> *Olympus, realm eternal Protégé of libidinous Zeus*
> *Snatched forever more from home.*
> *Perfection bestowed on you mortal child*
> *of beauty and tenderness*
> *Velvet soft and satin fine skin*
> *Soft unkempt hair wafting*
> *O'er youthful shoulders*
> *Eyes wide in anticipation and fear*
> *Fetch me some Ambrosia and deliver it*
> *to my chamber.*

The rest of the newspaper article quoted the opinions of two professors the reporter interviewed who were asked about the quality of Norman's poem. They were also asked if they thought that the poem seemed plagiarized. One professor said the poem was not of high caliber but was consistent with the writing of college students. The other professor refused to offer a comment on whether the poem was an original work.

Gary asked Clara Wright if she thought Norman might have plagiarized some his writing. Her response surprised Gary. "No, I don't believe he was into plagiarizing his work. Somewhere in his upbringing he was made aware of behavioral limits. Except on the few occasions when he tried to shock people, he was meticulously well behaved. If I left a one hundred dollar bill on a table and Norman was in the room alone with no one around, he wouldn't take it. I know it sounds strange, but I strongly feel he wasn't into cheating."

The newspaper reporter had found only one of Norman's writings and based on it assumed that Norman was fixated on death and human pain and anguish. Gary was interested in locating some of his other writings to see if they revealed such themes.

Searching the police files Gary found several other Norman creations, including a poem that described his feelings when he got drunk, two other mythological poems that described man as an insect who needed to die and leave the earth, and a short story entitled, *The Visitor*, in which Norman described himself as an alien who was sent to earth to be with his brothers to help them avoid a catastrophe that would destroy them.

His writings were indeed dark and macabre. He wrote specifically about out of body experiences, death and dying, and coping with human pain. Apparently, his childhood Dark Shadows fascination continued as he grew into adulthood with his writing and thinking becoming more grotesque as he developed a personal desire to experience first hand the thrill of inflicting pain and suffering on innocent people. It appeared that he had a growing need for power and control over helpless others as a way of striking back at his tormentors and showing his personal superiority. Unfortunately, defenseless young children were his chosen prey.

Norman described some of his own torment in his writing. One section was particularly revealing where he talked about voices flashing through his brain disconnected, flashes that were never ending and driving him to hell.

His fixation with death and the futility of life was quite apparent. He wrote about insects waiting to be squashed and living out their lives in pain, wanting peace to come again. He felt men were but puppets on strings waiting to die.

In reading his narratives, Gary was reminded of a comment made by Jeffrey Dahmer in an interview explaining how he became a born-again Christian while in prison. He said that prior to his alleged conversion, Dahmer believed man came from slime and returned to slime. Norman appeared to share similar feelings believing that man had little control over his actions while on earth.

One of Norman's professors told Gary that at one time Norman had became infatuated with an attractive female theatre student who had a steady boyfriend. Her boyfriend was also in theatre and a guy that Norman clearly disliked. The pretty young woman was soft-spoken, encouraging and kind to Norman, and he spent as much time in her company as possible, especially when her boyfriend was not around. She also was the only classmate who attended Norman's unsuccessful college auditions and his off campus Community Theatre plays.

In his short story, *The Visitor*, Norman wrote with particular sensitivity about his love for a girl named Peggy, whom he must leave behind as he returns to his home world, called Argos Talosia.

Interestingly, Norman describes Peggy as being a girl who gave him a most unusual feeling. He feared the terrible pain he might suffer if he were to leave her behind. Although he has been ordered home to Argos Talosia, he resists, refusing to leave his loved one. By staying, he now feels complete, especially when Peggy presents him with a son. He describes the peace and exultation he now feels as overwhelming.

Quite honestly, Gary didn't know what to make of Norman's display of feeling for Peggy. Most of the time, it was apparent that Norman felt like a piece of trash, angry at the world for rejecting him. But here in his short story, Gary saw Norman yearning for a woman, someone who loves him even though he is an alien from another planet. One wonders if Peggy is the college girl who befriended and reached out to Norman, encouraged him, and made him feel worthwhile—obviously a special young lady to whom he could talk to and let into his tortured world. In his story, he is clearly screaming for normalcy in his life, to be rid of his gross exterior and warped personality. He describes that special joy and pride in being a father for the first time. Reading his show of emotion, it makes it even more puzzling that a few years later, he tried to kill again.

Chapter 50

The last person Gary interviewed was Norman's college advisor, Professor Trudy Light. Trudy had Norman in several of her classes and had a lengthy involvement with him during his nearly three years in college. She agreed to meet Gary for an extended lunch at the college faculty club, where they managed to find a quiet spot to discuss Norman and his college experience.

Trudy was a tall, attractive, perky woman in her late fifties whom Gary had previously met when they served together on a state committee a few years back. Trudy's reputation was well known on campus—she was a dedicated, creative teacher who as an instructor and advisor went out of her way to help her students.

Trudy also had a background in sociology, particularly in observing aberrant behavior. She freely admitted that in over thirty years of teaching, there were only two students she considered to be dangerous to themselves and to others, and Norman was one of them.

Like Dan Fredericks, she had seen Norman for the first time in the play where he bolted out from under the pile of leaves. She also thought at the time, "Something is not right about a person who would stay that long under a bunch of leaves; it is not a healthy thing."

Gary was curious and asked Trudy why she thought Norman was a dangerous person.

"I had a lot of interaction with Norman and observed him closely while he was with us. It was quite apparent to me that he had an obsession with children. Occasionally I would bring my two young children to work with me and I would always ask someone to keep their eye on Norman because I was fearful of having him approach my kids. He made me uncomfortable, and then he kept hounding me and asking if he could babysit my kids. However, several of my fellow professors, against my advice, did hire him as a babysitter. I told them they were crazy, warning them that he was dangerous, but several of them used him anyway. All the time I dealt with Norman I didn't want him to pay attention to my children and me. Although I was his advisor, I kept him at a distance. He really scared me."

Gary asked, "How did you find him when you met with him as his advisor?"

"It was a strained relationship. Norman was a social outcast who didn't fit the norm. He was separated from others by his physical appearance. This was before obesity was treated like it is now, a disease. He enjoyed theatre because he could be someone else. He saw the world only in terms of himself and completely lacked empathy for others. Getting him to talk clearly was a serious problem.

" He deliberately reasoned so much in his head that he couldn't get the original sounds and his own thoughts out. He combined aberrant behavior with a fixation for death. After awhile, I thought he was more a danger to others than to himself.

"I didn't see Norman as suicidal but I thought he needed counseling and urged him to go to the counseling center. In fact, after I received several calls from people who thought he might have been stalking some girls and some young boys, I called the counseling center myself and told them about Norman, but they said it had to be a self-referral and not a referral by someone else. He was also like a ghost most of the time, invisible, but then suddenly he would do something shocking to bring attention to himself."

"What shocking things are you talking about?"

"Well, one time he sat in class and exposed himself. He had deliberately cut the seam in the crotch of his pants. He didn't wear any underwear and as a result exposed his genitals to his classmates and to me. He was facing me and making a statement, 'This is what I am going to do or please stop me.' I had to privately read him the riot act and told him he was lucky I didn't have him arrested. I then told him to go to the costume shop immediately and get that seam sewed up.

"Realizing the young man needed professional help, I again called the counseling center and insisted that somehow we had to get Norman into counseling. Unfortunately, it never happened."

Trudy had another incident she wanted to tell Gary. It concerned Norman's strong desire to have her accept some of his writing.

"We let students write scripts and if they were good enough we would produce them. One day, Norman approached me with a stack of papers with things he had written that he thought could be used to enhance one of the student plays we were producing. He said his script could be used to enrich and extend some of the scenes where murder and death were the central focus.

"I thanked him and explained we didn't need his suggestions at this point because we had finished with rewriting and editing the script and were ready to go forward with the play. To this day, I wonder if those sheets were the same ones the police seized in his bedroom. They might have been because he was at a point where I really think it didn't matter to him if he got caught or not."

"What makes you say that?"

Trudy paused and took a sip of her coffee. "I truly feel that Norman was tortured so much while in college that that he was willing to risk getting caught in order to satisfy his repressed sexual needs and to strike back at those who rejected him by committing another shocking act of violence.

"Norman definitely became more brazen as he confronted a series of disappointments while in college. His inner rage obviously grew and grew, but he disguised it well. He became this other person, an alter ego, who looked strange and did strange things while hiding the real Norman, the desperate man whose sexual appetite and rage were about to go out of control. Unfortunately, it was just a matter of time before he killed again and it didn't matter who it was the second time around. He was a very sick young man, very sick."

"Was this the situation when he killed Justin?" Gary asked.

"No it wasn't. Although you said he stated in his confession that he killed at random and it just happened to be Justin, I don't believe him. It was more a planned and deliberate killing. However, he was at a different point at age twenty-three in his desperateness than he was at sixteen. I am convinced that in 1982 it could have been any boy or young man in the neighborhood or somewhere else in town. Donnie Richmond just happened to be available that day. Although he asked him repeatedly to have a drink with him, he had also asked other young kids the same thing.

"In attempting to kill Donnie, he was more spontaneous in his actions and not as deliberate in his methods. He acted more in the moment without a lot of prior thought or advanced planning. Not so with Justin. In Justin, he saw himself and actually was killing himself. You know what I mean, 'This child is me and I am this child.'"

Hearing that, Gary said, "Trudy isn't that a bit farfetched?"

"No it isn't. Think about it for a moment. Justin was shy, withdrawn, and had a lisp, the same as Norman. He saw himself and was experiencing death through Justin. It was going to be some sort of thrill, some fun. He was too much of a coward to commit suicide. When he killed Justin, Norman was on a thrill ride constructing his own perfect crime and cleverly fooling people for a long time in a series of very complex maneuvers, such as boiling and hiding the body and disposing of all remains except for his trophy skull and bones.

"As I said previously, it was just the opposite with Donnie Richmond, where it was a spur of the moment thing where his testosterone went wacky. If he hadn't acted impulsively and tried to strangle Donnie, he may never have been caught.

"So that is the basis of my thinking—in 1982, he didn't care if he got caught or not. He was ready to take incredible risks. Of course, he was scared about what would happen to him after he was incarcerated, but he was so desperate and filled with pent-up rage and brimming with anger that he felt killing Donnie was worth the risk of getting caught."

Gary was interested in her last statement, "What makes you feel Norman was on a thrill ride?"

"He said as much in his confession when he said he killed the boy because it was some kind of fun."

"Yes, that's true, but Trudy, can you believe him?"

"Why would he lie at that point? You have to remember that Norman was fascinated by Greek mythology and fantasized about the rituals of human sacrifice practiced by the Olympian gods. This fascination occurred early in his youth long before college. When he was in college he actually gave me one of his morbid essays he had written in high school.

"His fixation with mythology and with death and dying lead me to believe that when he stabbed Justin he was reenacting some fantasy in his mind where he was an Olympian god. Although he had an intense interest in death and dying he may have actually been fearful of death at that point in his life. Justin therefore was being sacrificed in place of him. He thought it would be fun to do something like killing a small child, seeking the thrill I alluded to.

"I know this may be hard for you to believe, but remember Norman was a really disturbed and dangerous young man. He was a full blown sadistic sexual psychopath without a sense of moral responsibility and social conscience."

Gary's head was spinning as he assimilated Trudy's theories. "You are way out there now, Trudy. To me it sounds like psychoanalysis overload. I suppose you have heard the rumors about what Norman did to Justin's body."

Trudy responded quickly, "You mean the stuff about how he allegedly boiled and ate part of the boy's remains and performed a sex act on the dead body?"

"Yes," Gary said. "That information has leaked out and has not been refuted by anyone who has read the infamous sealed journal where Norman provides what the police believe are lurid details of the actual killing."

Trudy's face tightened. "I hate to admit it but it probably is true. I know it is evil in the worst form, but Norman was a desperate young man. There are a number of stories in Greek mythology that involve cannibalism. Norman read widely and as I said earlier it would not surprise me if he were reenacting some scene from some play he read trying to experience what it would be like to eat human flesh."

The idea was making Gary feel nauseous, but he had to ask Trudy the next question. "What about the rumor concerning his practice of necrophilia?"

"I know little about necrophilia, but what I do know fits nicely with why he also may have had sex with a dead body. A necrophile usually has poor self-esteem, many times due in part to a significant loss. I understand Norman lost his mother at a young age and it affected him deeply. A necrophile is usually male and very fearful of rejection by women, which again was the case with Norman. They desire a sexual object that is incapable of rejecting them since they have a need to express their power over a corpse."

"Trudy, you know more than I will ever know or want to know," Gary said.

"Not really. The research on necrophilia is pretty sketchy. I know a little about it because I was in a play once where one of the actors played that particular role and had more information about that despicable practice than I wanted to hear. One line he had in the play has stuck with me for a long time. Again, it relates to Norman's situation. The character blamed his desire to have sex with a corpse as an evil curse. He said something like, 'This curse has followed me all my life. I try to suppress my uncontrollable desire, but I cannot. This filthy curse has resulted in my self-destructiveness and a hatred of life.'"

Still feeling nauseous, Gary changed the subject before Trudy went any further and started telling him about the cannibalism references in Shakespeare's *Twelfth Night* and the myth of Saturn devouring his children. He couldn't believe that we were talking about Norman Stedman of Hopeville, Massachusetts, her former student and his having committed one of the most evil crimes in the history of our state.

"One last question for you, Trudy. Why did Norman drop out of school?"

"Probably due to disappointment and the fact that his dream of becoming a professional actor was crumbling. I tried to help him and talked to him about other career options. I urged him to get professional help and told him if he did I would go to bat for him, like I would do for any of my students, and try to get him placed in another department with a different major. On the other hand, I had to be honest with him and tell him that he just wasn't talented enough to be a successful actor. He left school shortly after that conversation."

"Trudy, do you have anything else you would like to add?"

"Yes, I never knew that Norman lived across the street from Justin Doherty. I didn't realize he did until after his arrest. If I had known, I most likely would have had a private conversation with the police regarding their need to closely check him out."

Chapter 51

After his talk with Trudy Light, Gary was perplexed. Although he initially thought Trudy was overanalyzing Norman's anti-social personality, upon reflection much of what she had said may not have been that farfetched. Her insights were related to Norman having a mental illness, to his being, in her words, "a full blown sadistic sexual psychopath."

That was a mouthful, but it did raise a question in Gary's mind: If Norman was that seriously ill, why didn't his lawyer follow through on his original intention of entering a "not guilty by reason of insanity" plea? This confused Gary. In 1982, state psychiatrists found Norman capable of standing trail and not being insane, whatever "insane" meant back then.

A week after their first conversation, he called Trudy Light and asked her if she could help him. Trudy had just finished dinner with her family and it sounded like she was still munching on something.

"Trudy, I'm sorry to bother you. I didn't mean to interrupt your dinner."

"No problem, Gary. We had a late dinner and just finished. What can I do for you?"

Gary explained the reason for his call and asked her if she knew of anyone who could provide an answer to his question about what constitutes insanity.

"I do know a psychiatrist at McLean Hospital in Boston who might be able to shed some light on your question. His name is Dr. Elliot Katz, an old family friend, who has had considerable experience in working with juvenile psychopaths, several of whom were murderers and are currently receiving psychiatric care at several prison hospitals. If you would like, I can contact him and set up a meeting for you in the near future."

"That's great, Trudy. Many thanks."

"You will enjoy Elliot. He is exceptionally bright and has an outstanding reputation in the Boston area and beyond. He will probably tell you that when state medical officials assess the mental condition of criminals, detection of a serious mental illness rarely occurs. Hopefully, Elliot can explain why that generally seems to be the case."

Two weeks passed before Gary received a call from Dr. Katz's secretary and the following Wednesday, Gary found himself battling Boston traffic. In spite of having visited the hospital several times while teaching in Boston, he got lost, barely arriving in time for his appointment.

The reception area in Katz's office was a pleasant surprise after observing the depressing exterior of the hospital buildings. Fresh cut flowers, three massive, glowing tropical fish tanks, a gallery of colorful framed prints on soft tan walls, plush crème colored carpeting and comfortable deep brown leather chairs and sofa bordered with fine teak tables created a special warmth and comfort. A young, tastefully dressed receptionist with a stylish blond coiffure escorted Gary into Katz's plush office. Katz sprang from his leather desk chair and greeted him enthusiastically with a firm handshake.

"Gary, so nice to meet you. Trudy told me about your research project and possible book. You have taken on a fascinating case that sounds extremely complex.

"It has been a challenge getting the facts, Dr. Katz. Hopefully, you can help me clarify a couple of questions that have surfaced. I realize that there are patient-doctor privilege issues, but I would like to know how Norman Stedman, who both Trudy and I felt was severely mentally ill, was not declared insane when he was arrested over twenty-five years ago. I also wonder about the possibility of his rehabilitation in prison, but I realize all we can do is speculate about that."

As Katz sat down on his couch facing him, Gary took a good look at him. He had to be in his late sixties, but could pass for much younger. He was a short and stocky man with a hairline that obviously had disappeared years ago leaving white peach fuzz on his shiny head. He had a youthful looking face that reminded him of the pudgy, round face of the late actor, John Candy, albeit attached to a smaller body.

"Those are not easy questions to answer, Gary. If you don't mind, I would like to rephrase your question. You need to ask me, 'When is a criminal's mental illness serious enough to warrant treatment, yet not serious enough to completely absolve him of his criminal responsibility?'"

"Yes, that's exactly what I want to know."

"Great, here is my take. I talked with Trudy about Norman Stedman when she called last week and I agree with her. If the rumors surrounding the case are true as you say they are then Stedman is clearly a psychopathic sexual sadist with possible extreme fetishes of sexualized cannibalism and necrophilia. His problems are deep-rooted and very rare even among serial killers. His sexual fantasies appear to be focused on dead bodies where he would face no resistance and be in complete control, unlike in his real life where he was obviously physically repulsive and constantly rejected and sexually deprived. It is fortunate the paperboy woke up when he did before Stedman had killed him and then satisfied his perverse sexual appetite.

"Although I would have to read Stedman's case file in detail and talk with the professionals who evaluated him, but based on my discussion with Trudy, my initial feeling is that Stedman is similar to many serial killers and can be best classified as an anti-social psychopath. In my experience, I have found two different sociopath personalities. First, there is the Ted Bundy type who was very cunning and charming and more of the guy-next-door type. Norman is the other type—the loner, the anti-social personality with serious and complex problems. Unlike the Bundy type, Stedman's type is not as organized and cunning. They are more disorganized, leave clues, and usually are easier to catch."

Gary thought this was true of the attack on Donnie Richmond, but not the murder of Justin Doherty. "But, Dr. Katz, Norman meticulously planned the kidnapping and murder of Justin Doherty. It took the police about seven years to catch him and when they did it was pretty much luck."

"Yes, it may have looked like a well-conceived plan, but from what Trudy told me it wasn't. Critical evidence was left in his bedroom and subject to discovery. It apparently was easy to fool his father and the other relatives in his house. I understand that his father was a respected former policeman whose word was trusted. And finally, the local police lacked experience with such crimes and made some significant investigative mistakes. Given those conditions, Norman's high level of intelligence allowed him to cover up a crime for all those years until he couldn't resist the driving need to kill again."

Gary asked Katz if he was familiar with the research of criminologists Ressler, Burgess, and Douglas when they wrote about sexual homicide patterns and motives and the" totem phase" that some serial killers go through with their victims.

"Of course, I am. You are wondering if Stedman fits this category like Dahmer does, aren't you?"

Gary had to confess, "Yes, I am. But realize it may be a stretch.

"Not necessarily. Stedman may have been so depressed that he sought sadistic sexual satisfaction and control over living victims' bodies since it is known that he did cut up the body and develop a ritual to preserve his success by keeping news clippings, photos, and parts of the victim's body or show parts of the bodies to other possible victims. He also left a journal that apparently describes other despicable things he did to the dead boy's body. Let's pray that he didn't cannibalize body parts or sexually exploit the young boy after he killed him.

"Similar to Dahmer, Stedman's trophies probably gave him the same feelings he experienced at the time of the kill. So I feel there is considerable merit to the theories of the criminologists you reference."

Gary had more questions. "So, if Norman apparently didn't have a compulsive schizoid personality disorder, does this mean it was easier for the state medical doctors to find him competent to stand trail? Is that what you're saying?" Gary inquired.

"Exactly," Katz said. "Criminals who are clearly psychotic out of touch with reality and not of sane mind are more likely to be found incompetent to stand trial than types like Stedman who realize exactly what they are doing when they kill. It might have been a very easy call for state psychiatrists, especially if they hadn't read his journal, where he provided specific details about how he violated the young boy's dead body. Do you know if the psychiatrists actually read the journal?"

"I don't think they did, but his lawyer did."

"Gary, you can't blame his lawyer for agreeing to the plea bargain. Realizing that an insanity plea was fruitless, he opted for a reduced sentence with the possibility for parole. If you ask me, it was a pretty good deal, too good to turn down."

"What makes you say that?" Gary countered.

"Today life imprisonment without parole seems to be the typical sentence given for crimes as heinous as Norman's. This is the new standard. Norman's crime definitely reached this highest level of heinousness," Katz explained.

"What about 1982?" Gary asked.

"I'm not as sure about 1982. I have been in this field for over forty years and I have seen some obvious changes in thinking especially in the sentencing of psychopath killers.

The political winds have shifted. The public's dissatisfaction with the loopholes in the insanity laws has forced a new sentencing standard that has been strongly supported by the media, law enforcement officials, and legislators.

"It is now very difficult for lawyers to prove that their clients were insane when they committed capital crimes since they must establish, for instance, that the killer clearly didn't know what he was doing when he or she committed the ghastly murderous act. Again, if the crime was extremely heinous, lawyers are now pleading 'Guilty, but mentally ill' which provides their clients with psychiatric treatment in a prison hospital."

"Isn't this the same thing that happened to Norman?" Gary asked.

"Yes, but there is a big difference. In such cases, the sentences are life imprisonment without parole, not a reduced sentence with the possibility of parole like Norman got. The focus is now primarily on public protection. A good illustration is Jeffrey Dahmer. Suppose he was found insane, received treatment, and was released to society after a few short years. Can you imagine the public outcry and the media frenzy this would have caused?"

"What about that fifteen-year-old Oregon boy, Kip something or other?" Gary asked.

Katz knew all about that case. "His name was Kip Kinkel. If you recall in 1998 he killed his mother and father in his home and the next day entered his school cafeteria and killed two students and injured twenty-five others. He was tried as an adult and sentenced to 111 years in prison without parole."

Katz continued his explanation, "The Kinkel case demonstrates what I was talking about. The boy was under treatment for a short period of time, but unfortunately his therapy was discontinued abruptly. His sentence was an illustration of what we now do to criminals who commit heinous crimes of this nature. We warehouse them. They killed, so warehouse them at great taxpayer expense until they die. The focus is on retribution and incapacitation, and less on rehabilitation."

"I gather that you think rehabilitation in prison is not that effective?" Gary said.

"Unfortunately, you're right. We do a lousy job of psychiatric and psychosocial rehabilitation. It's more than a case of not having enough money to hire qualified medical personnel. It's also an attitude. Prisons by their very nature are punitive institutions, especially for juveniles. Public protection is our top priority and somehow people have to understand that rehabilitation is a vital part of the protection equation and needs to be valued more than it has been. We have to do more than give prisoners anti-depressants, and we do, but rehabilitation is not the priority it should be. The public perception fed by the media is that all that we are doing is giving inmates Prozac every day to calm them down."

Gary felt like an intern getting clinical feedback from Katz as the good doctor further expounded, "We have to give greater attention to thorough care of the young mentally ill in our society. The lack of effective youth treatment is a real problem today with increased stress and conflict due to the rising number of broken homes, sexual assaults, and alcohol and drug addiction cases."

"Isn't part of the problem one of better detection and referral policies?" Gary asked. "For example, Norman cleverly hid his mental problems and refused counseling."

"Yes, Trudy told me that. Unfortunately, mental illness is still a pervasive stigma that not only troubled youth hide but their families do as well. A sociopath with Norman's profile blames others for his problems. They are in constant denial. In late 70's, few school districts had full-time school psychologists or referred students for help unless they were extreme cases affecting the safety of the school or were suicidal in nature.

"We hear about the Kip Kinkels in the sensational newspaper articles and television snips, but what isn't reported is the number of cases where identification, intervention, referral, counseling, and therapy have actually worked for thousands of our youth. Hopefully, we are making progress in these areas as the stigma of mental illness lessens."

As they shook hands and walked into his reception area, Gary thanked Dr. Katz for his time and information. He wished Gary well on his research and encouraged him to write his book.

Gary took a final look at this small, heavy-set man in his white coat and large black-framed glasses and thought about the number of mentally disturbed sexual offenders he must have treated during his long career as a psychiatrist. How many were rehabilitated successfully, released from prison, and went on to lead normal lives? He wondered if Katz knew. He can't imagine working all those years without some validation of his life's work.

Before he went out the door, Gary asked Dr. Katz two quick questions. "Do you think Norman was on his way to becoming a serial killer if he hadn't been caught?"

"There is a good possibility he would have killed again given his pattern," Katz explained. "I can't say that with any degree of certainty without interviewing him and thoroughly reading his record; however, he was at the age when serial killers create multiple murders—in their late twenties and early thirties. If he had employment, transportation and started living independently who knows what he would have done? He was obviously a very dangerous person."

Gary had one last question. "After talking with Trudy and what you know about Norman, what are his chances for rehabilitation and release after so many years in prison?"

With a slight smirk on his face, Katz replied, "I wouldn't put my money on it. His problems seem very deep-rooted to me."

When he finally found his car in the hospital's massive parking lot, Gary reflected on Katz's final comment. He thought, "Nobody has the answers to how a mentally ill person like Norman can be rehabilitated".

Chapter 52

Having completed his revealing research on Norman Stedman and what may have motivated him to turn into a child killer, Gary was compelled to learn what effect his crime had on the police, on the people in the community, and on members of the Doherty and Richmond families.

He had just found an old copy of a May 1982 newspaper article in the *Hopeville Times* with a headline that read, *"Detective Sadly Ends All Consuming Case."* It was time for Gary to interview someone he knew many years ago, Rick Thurston.

Thurston was now in his early seventies and had been retired from the police force for over twenty-five years. He agreed to have breakfast with Gary at the Hopeville Diner, once a popular tourist spot, but now just another local hangout where the home fries are so greasy you had to separate them from eggs and toast on your plate with a napkin.

After a breakfast of lumpy buttermilk pancakes, they sat in the parking lot in the quiet of Gary's car. He looked closely at Rick Thurston. The years had been good to him. He still had his boyish charm and looked in fine physical shape, although his face showed a few more wrinkles and his graying hair was starting to thin. He surely looked younger than other grandfathers around town. Still working part time as a private investigator, he was anxious to talk about the Justin Doherty case.

"Rick, there are three rumors relating to the Doherty case that won't go away. I would like your take on them."

"Shoot," he said.

"People are still saying that you didn't search the Stedman house because Fred Stedman had been a reserve police officer and you automatically took his word."

"That's not quite true. Yes, we didn't do our own physical search inside any of the houses on the street except the Doherty's house and two apartments in the project. Out buildings and cellars were also searched by local firemen."

Gary asked him to explain what procedures were actually followed in searching the other houses.

"You have to remember," Rick said. "This was a close knit neighborhood. We were looking to see if Justin might have been inside someone's house. At that time we didn't think that someone in the neighborhood had kidnapped him or he had been taken him out of town. We were not looking for a dead boy's body at that time or even later for that matter."

"Chuck Harrison told me that you went to every house on the street, knocked on the door, and asked the owner whether they had done a thorough search of their house. If they hadn't, you asked them to do one. Is that correct?"

"Yes, it is. I remember going to the Stedman house. Fred came to the door and Norman was standing behind him nervously twitching as usual. We asked Fred if he had checked all the rooms in his house and he said he had. He turned to Norman and asked if he had checked the cellar and outside shed and Norman said he had."

"Todd Jenks told me that the firemen checked the cellars, yards, cesspools, and sheds and that he personally checked the Stedman cellar, but he didn't see any trunks."

"That's true," Rick said. "All he probably did was take a quick look."

"So let me get this right. Even if you did know Fred from past associations, the fact that he had been a reserve policeman was not a factor in your decision to personally search his house? In other words, you followed the same procedure at every house on the street including the Stedman house."

"That's right. It was more a mistake in police procedure than anything else. We should have done our own physical search of every house on the street. Looking back, it is a mistake I greatly regret."

Gary was taken back by his comment. He wondered if he felt that way twenty-five years ago and said, "Twenty-twenty hindsight is wonderful. Still left unanswered is what Norman did with Justin's body in the first few days of the search. If the body wasn't in the trunk where was it? As you think about the case after all these years, do you think the body was locked up in his bedroom closet in a plastic bag as Norman claimed or was it in the trunk pushed into the crawl space out of sight in the cellar?"

Rick shook his head. "How would I know? Only Norman really knows and you can't believe what he says. You can't ask Fred either, because he's dead. We will never know the answer to that question."

"I heard another rumor that won't go away and I am sure you have heard it many times. How could Norman have done the things he did without Fred learning at some point in time that he had killed Justin?"

Rick's tone suddenly changed and his voice softened, "I understand why people find it hard to believe that he didn't know. But the people who said those things didn't know Fred like I did. In fact, few people really knew him. He was a quiet, unassuming, nice guy who kept to himself.

"People also don't know anything about his relationship with Norman, except I knew that Fred didn't know what to do with him. These people weren't present when he broke down when we told him we thought his son had killed Justin. Believe me, it was no act. Velone also questioned him at length. He also believed that Fred was being truthful in his statement when he said he didn't know his son was involved in Justin's disappearance until the moment we asked him to search his house."

"But Rick, how could Norman not be suspected while he and two other adults lived in that little house? Who knows, his grandmother or mother may have known and even told Fred."

"We had no evidence that Fred's mother or his wife knew anything about Norman killing Justin. It is possible Norman left the body covered in the cellar trunk and didn't touch it until after the two women had died. This might explain some of the smell.

"Look, I knew Fred as well as anyone. He went on patrol with me many times. It does not surprise me that Norman could very easily con Fred. To be honest with you, Fred was not that sharp. If he was, he wouldn't have gone all those years smelling as badly as he did."

Gary then asked a sensitive question. "I know you have heard the rumors that Norman may have had sex with Justin's dead body and ate parts either before or after he finished boiling the body. He then shellacked the skull and remaining bones and kept them as mementos. The Judge's sealing of the journal and the strong denial of my request by correction officials to communicate with Norman point to the fact that he did some pretty sick things to Justin's body. When you consider that based upon what they read in the journal, Harrison and Velone feel strongly that Norman is incapable of rehabilitation and should remain in prison for life. This leads me to believe that there is some substance to the cannibalism and necrophilia rumors. Is that a reasonable assumption on my part?"

Rick reluctantly admitted, "Yes, that it is a reasonable assumption."

Gary then asked, "Do you feel that Norman's journal account is mainly fictional as he claims it is?"

"It definitely is not fictional. When you read his journal and compare what he said he did to the boy against the evidence we gathered, it matches up. Although he said he didn't write his journal until around 1980, the notes he used to write his despicable account we know through our scientific analysis were written several years before that. His contention that the passage of time led to embellishments in his journal is pure hogwash!"

Gary wanted to know the effect the Doherty case had on Rick's career. He chose his words carefully. "I need to ask you a few personal questions about your involvement in the case. You obviously loved being a policeman and had a nice career. You retired a bit early and I wondered if the Doherty case may have influenced your decision to retire when you did."

Rick thought for a moment before answering. "You're right. I loved being a cop and particularly enjoyed being a detective. I had ambitions of some day being appointed chief and when Chief Sawyer retired, I applied for the job and didn't get it. I don't know if some slip-ups we had during the seven years we were looking for Justin had anything to do with being passed over or not. I doubt it. It probably had more to do with the town wanting to make a complete change from the past and hiring an outsider with new ideas and different experience.

"It doesn't really matter and it does no good to look back. I am not a bitter guy. I do know one thing and that is I did the very best I could under the circumstances for the Doherty family and Jane appreciated that. That's the important thing to me. I had a great career in Hopeville even though it soured a little at the end."

As they parted company, Gary watched Rick drive away in his

maroon colored sports car and thought how unpredictable life is. When a tragedy hits a small community, it affects everyone in some way, and some more than others. Detective Rick Thurston's career and reputation had been on the line, but he survived and now he could hold his head high. He gave a most valiant effort, above and beyond the normal course of duty.

Chapter 53

Gary learned that when the macabre nature of Norman's crime was revealed to residents after his arrest in 1982, it generated considerable fear throughout the community. He called Jerry O'Reilly one day and asked if he could interview him because someone had told him that he had a story to tell about how community fear doesn't just evaporate after a tragedy, but lingers for some time.

O'Reilly was a popular, jocular, heavy-set Irishman, who for years had served as a state probation officer. Upon retirement, he was elected to the state General Assembly as the representative for Hopeville.

Before he told Gary his story, O'Reilly wanted him to know that he had met with Norman Stedman shortly after his arrest in his professional capacity as a probation officer. This was something Gary didn't know and he was anxious to gather O'Reilly's perceptions of Norman along with his story about how fear can affect a community.

O'Reilly was assigned to prepare a pre-sentence report on Norman for the court and interviewed him twice while he was at the IMH holding center awaiting trial.

He said, "I found Norman uncommunicative, uttering only one or two word responses to the questions I asked him. He also didn't appear remorseful except for one emotionless 'I'm sorry' response. He was a tough guy to reach."

O'Reilly told Gary that Norman had no previous record with the police or the state juvenile division and had been employed part-time with some success. Although unemployed in 1982, he was still active in the local theatre and, as O'Reilly said with the command of the English language only the Irish have, "Where he could shed the hunchback, disheveled persona that people witnessed as he walked the streets of Hopeville and enter the world of make-believe." Although Norman was odd, O'Reilly admitted that he found no record of deviant behavior.

"My report to the court was therefore very brief and perfunctory," he said.

O'Reilly also offered another interesting piece of information that spoke to the severity of Norman's crime. He explained that Norman was prosecuted and sentenced as an adult rather than as a sixteen-year-old juvenile when he had killed Justin. He told Gary that Kenny, McCaffrey and Judge Griffin had reached a private agreement in the plea bargain to waive Norman out of the juvenile system and Family Court and try him as an adult in Superior Court. That action was similar to the procedure used a few years later in a Rhode Island case in which a sixteen-year-old juvenile violently killed a mother and her two daughters in their home.

As he reflected on the brutal murder of Justin Doherty, O'Reilly remembered an experience that illustrated the fear and anxiety that remained among townspeople years after Norman was incarcerated:

"It was about 1989 when I got an anxious call from the Hopeville police. Apparently, they had received a number of calls from terrified people who had seen Norman walking the streets of Hopeville again. I quickly called the Department of Corrections and was told that Norman was clearly still in an undisclosed out of state facility and had not been released. I breathed a deep sigh of relief.

"Later that evening my wife and I were driving home from a social gathering when at the corner of Oak and High Street, I saw this hulking, hunchback fellow with black rimmed glasses and beard stumbling along. Before I got out of my car, I told my wife to call the police or 911 if anything went wrong. When I approached the guy, he was the spitting image of Norman. I quickly told him why it wasn't a good idea for him to remain in Hopeville unless he changed his clothes, shaved off his beard and took off his glasses."

Gary didn't ask O'Reilly if he gently told the fellow to consider leaving town as soon as practicable, but knowing his penchant for candor, he wouldn't be surprised if he suggested that the poor guy quickly catch a bus out of town before he got a bullet in his head. Even given his noted frugality and deep pockets, O'Reilly would have probably have paid the bus fair.

Chapter 54

Victims of a capital crime often find it difficult to put the horrors of the crime behind them and get on with their lives. Healing is a lifelong process. This was particularly true for the Doherty and Richmond families.

The plea bargain agreement reached in the sentencing of Norman clearly didn't help them gain closure. Their suffering did not end after the court decision or Justin's funeral; unfortunately, it was relived in all its intensity when Norman was granted a parole hearing in 1992.

After having served ten years in prison, the minimum amount of time an inmate of a capital crime must serve before being eligible for a hearing, Norman had requested one. Jane, her daughter Robin, and friends of the Doherty family circulated petitions throughout the Hopeville area to keep Norman behind bars. Approximately five thousand signatures were gathered from a dozen stores and restaurants.

Chief Velone, Jane and Robin were prepared to give testimony, but George Doherty feared it would be too upsetting for him to attend. "It hurts too much to think about it," George told the press. He planned to write a letter to the board stating his opposition to freeing Norman from jail.

The state Attorney General also planned to attend the hearing to argue against freeing Norman because of the "gruesome and atrocious" nature of the crime.

Velone told Gary that he sought permission from Judge Griffin to read excerpts from Norman's journal. He gave Gary a copy of the request he had sent to the judge, which read: "My request to you is to allow me to utilize excerpts from Mr. Stedman's journal in conjunction with my testimony so the parole board will have a very clear understanding as to all aspects of Justin Doherty's murder. I have previously discussed my possible testimony with the Dohertys and they have agreed to honor a request to leave the hearing while I give my testimony."

Velone went on to say that if members of the Parole Board objected to his reading the excerpts he would refrain from doing so.

Steve Jacobs, chairman of the Massachusetts Parole Board, told the press that it was unlikely that Norman would receive parole this early in his sentence. He said board policy in most cases is to refuse parole until about two-thirds of the sentence has been served—in Norman's case that would be in 2010, after he had served twenty-seven years. Only in unusual cases does the board deviate from its policy. He said an exception might be made if an inmate had a serious terminal illness and submitted supporting medical documentation to that effect.

Jacobs explained that Norman's hearing was being held in Massachusetts rather than in the state where he is presently incarcerated because of a law stating that when a prisoner voluntarily agrees to transfer to an undisclosed out of state correctional facility to better insure his personal safety, he remains a Massachusetts prisoner forever.

Gary learned that the parole board uses a national risk assessment instrument to help them determine if an inmate is a good candidate for parole. It asks board members a number of questions about the severity of the crime, the effect the crime has on the victims, the age of the inmate, the inmate's history while in prison, recommendations from psychiatrists, plans for home and work, and others subjects. Board members then assign weights to each factor. Jacobs said that it takes votes from four members of the six-member board to grant parole, and added, "In Mr. Stedman's case, the heinous nature of his crime would be an 'umbrella' that casts a negative shadow over the other factors in the assessment instrument."

Prior to the hearing, word was received that Norman would not be in attendance. The hearing was therefore held without him present.

After reading in the paper that Steve Jacobs was the Chairman of the Parole Board, Gary was anxious to talk to him about the hearing. Jacobs was one of his former college professors, a man he knew well. He wasted little time in picking up the phone and inviting Jacobs to lunch.

Chapter 55

Jacobs was a tall, distinguished, retired, seventy-six-year old African American and sociology professor who had served on the parole board for twenty-seven years, most of them as chairman. Not only did Gary want to hear his reaction to Norman's parole hearing but he also wanted to ask him to explain the parole process and why the Dohertys had to go through such mental torture every few years.

Gary met Jacobs for lunch at an upscale Italian restaurant in downtown Springfield. Jacobs greeted him with a cagey smile that Gary remembered from his undergraduate days when the professor enjoyed challenging his students and questioning their poorly formulated opinions. With his flowing silver hair and bushy mustache, he didn't look a day over 60. As they talked, Jacobs told him that he had seen almost everything during his time on the parole board, but the 1992 hearing for Norman Stedman was one he would never forget. Gary sensed that it was very difficult for the professor to reflect on what must have been a sad event.

Jacobs, in fact, ranked the experience as one of the most difficult and sad hearings he had ever attended. He then explained why. "Mrs. Doherty and her daughter were the only members of the family who attended the hearing and as is our custom we met privately with them prior to the formal hearing. Mrs. Doherty was a lovely woman and obviously quite nervous having to talk about the murder of her son once again, especially to a group of strangers. As we reviewed this tragic case with her, we saw the extreme agony on her face and our hearts went out to her.

Her daughter was more feisty and talkative, strongly stating the case why Stedman should never see 'the light of day' from his prison cell. Fortunately, Stedman chose not to testify, easing the tension we normally witness between family victims and the inmate.

"At the formal hearing, Chief Velone read some of the gruesome details from Stedman's journal to us and it made us sick. After awhile I told him to stop, we had heard enough. It was just awful, very awful! We denied Stedman parole and ruled that he would not be eligible for another hearing for five years. This was an unprecedented action because the Attorney General's Office favored giving another review hearing within a reasonable amount of time and most inmates can request another hearing after just a year.

I held a press conference after the hearing where I was peppered with questions from the media. I defended the board's decision saying it was one of the most barbaric crimes committed in Massachusetts history."

An emotional Jacobs told the reporters that, after reviewing the case and listening to the details from Norman's journal and as a father of three children, he was shocked that "a crime of this nature could be committed against a small child by another human being."

"I became teary-eyed and had to pause and compose myself before saying anything else. It was only the second time in two decades serving on the board that I lost my composure and broke down. The other time, the case also concerned a young child."

When the reporters pressed him further he said, "That's enough, that's it, I will say no more!"

After lunch, Gary asked Jacobs if Norman could be released from prison when two-thirds of his sentence is completed.

"Because of the severity of the inhuman crime he has committed, it is highly unlikely, although parole boards change over time and there is no sure thing," he told Gary.

"Could Norman be released before the completion of his sentence in 2023 if he accumulates good time?" Gary asked.

"Most definitely," Jacobs said. "The politicians are talking about eliminating good time and early release for sexual offenders, however, at this point Norman would receive good time. Because he was convicted in 1982 prior to passage of the sexual offender laws, he also would not be classified by the state as a sexual offender. It's hard to believe, but that's the case."

"How does good time work, Steve?"

"Well, good time is gained in prison if Stedman has not been disciplined and has a clean 'no problem' record. Conversely, he could accumulate 'bad time' as well for a number of infractions he may have committed and that would extend his time in prison time beyond his release date."

His explanation bothered Gary. "Knowing Norman's personality type, it is more likely he has accumulated more good time and very little, if any, bad time, unless of course he is provoked by other inmates who sense or learn that he is a 'diddler,' which I hear is inmate jargon for a child killer."

Jacobs agreed. "You definitely don't want to be known in the prison population as a diddler. Your life would be in constant danger. There is always some inmate in there looking to get their name in the paper claiming they got revenge for the boy and his family. Look at what happened to Jeffrey Dahmer when he was on a work detail in the prison gym and got his head smashed in."

Gary still needed to know more about good time. "With a forty-year sentence, couldn't Norman accumulate a considerable amount of good time?"

"Yes, he could. Maybe a few years or so."

"So, Norman might not request another parole hearing knowing that it would be futile," Gary surmised. "His best bet could be to keep accumulating good time and get released prior to 2023."

"Who knows," said the white-haired veteran board chair. "Time will tell, I guess."

Chapter 56

Norman did request another parole hearing in 1997. This time around, Jane, Robin and their supporters again gathered well over five thousand signatures in their petition drive. Chief Velone once again received authority to read excerpts from Norman's journal and George Doherty again decided not to attend the hearing. But there was one major difference—a few days before the scheduled hearing date Norman requested that it be cancelled.

The secretary of the parole board said she had received a call from Norman, who tersely stated, "I don't have time to properly prepare for the hearing and I will be denied anyway."

A few days after the cancellation of the hearing, a letter to the editor written by Robin Doherty appeared in the Hopeville Times. Robin wrote it in response to a previous letter to the editor written by a local minister. She didn't mince any words:

Norman Stedman acted on his own free will, and no one, not even Norman, has an excuse. Therapy in prisons may be minimal, but do you honestly think that any therapy would cure a killer? His soul has been lost, Reverend. In the end, God will decide- not me, not the courts, not you, only God.

I am no longer a child. I am a mother with a ten-year-old child. I don't want pity for my family or myself. We are survivors. We have not come through any of this unscathed.

There are wounds that will never heal, but we hold on to those things that are sacred and we pray.

I have no sympathy for Norman. I feel nothing for him at all. He is like a toothache, an uncomfortable reminder that something is wrong. My life has changed because of Norman's actions, and there is nothing he can do now to right his wrong. He has never shown remorse or guilt for taking the life of an innocent child, or attempting to take the life of another young man, who, although not related, was, and still is, a very dear part of our family.

Chapter 57

"We have not come through this unscathed. There are wounds that will never heal, but we hold on to those things that are sacred, and we pray," wrote Robin Doherty.

Her words made Gary think about the families that were victims of the atrocious crime committed by Norman. What has happened to them in the intervening years? The trauma of victimization is a direct reaction to the aftermath of a crime, but not everyone experiences the same reaction.

There are physical reactions like heart palpations and increased use of alcohol, as well as emotional reactions like grief, depression, anxiety and disorientation. In many cases, the effects of victimization are long lasting, even extending over thirty years, as in the case of those victimized by Justin Doherty's abduction and murder.

After her mother's funeral in September 2000, Robin changed her name and left Hopeville for parts unknown, after making arrangements with her brother, Joey, and his former wife, Diane, to take custody of her daughter. It was the last time her daughter and family members saw her.

Gary attempted to locate Robin through an Internet search, but was unsuccessful. She had moved quite often throughout the New England area. The telephone numbers listed for each one of her residences were no longer in operation. "We don't know where she is or what she is doing," said her disappointed and somewhat concerned brother, Joey.

George Doherty remarried eight years after Jane died from cancer. He became a successful businessman, owning and operating the appliance business that his mother and dad left him when they retired to Florida. George got out of appliance sales several years ago and now runs an appliance repair business with his son, Joey. George is still known, as he was by his Suffork Street neighbors, as "the man who can fix anything." He has also been active in the community, serving as an officer in a number of community organizations and as President of the Hopeville Fire Department.

But in spite of the appearance of normalcy in his life, George still has deep wounds from the memory of Justin's murder that time hasn't healed much at all. Gary learned this when he visited his appliance shop and asked George if he would be willing to grant him an interview.

As Gary entered the shop office slightly before 8 a.m., it was buzzing with activity. George and Joey stood behind the counter reviewing the day's paperwork they needed for their scheduled service calls. Used refrigerators, washers, and dryers were jammed into one corner and cardboard boxes containing recently arrived appliance parts were stacked haphazardly in back of the counter. Outside, cars hummed along Center Street as the people of Hopeville busily headed for work.

Diane, Joey's former wife and now the office secretary, warmly greeted Gary. She recognized Gary because her current husband had worked for years for the electrical contracting business run by Gary's brothers. Diane, George and Joey were the only ones in the small office at the time. Although divorced, she and Joey had an amicable relationship and good rapport.

Both George and Joey acknowledged Gary as he prepared to ask what he knew was an awkward question. He thought, "How do I put this?" Finally, he decided to come right out with it.

"Good morning, George," he said, looking directly at him and realizing that he was disrupting his busy early morning office routine. "I want to ask you if you would be willing to let me interview you regarding some research I am doing on Justin's murder case."

A deep chill quickly could be felt throughout the room. Joey and Diane each looked pained, and George's facial expression became almost ominous. Gary felt like he was standing there naked.

"I don't talk to anyone about Justin," he said.

"Oh, I understand that, George. That is your right and I respect that; however, I felt I needed to ask you. I want you to be the first to know that I may be writing a book about the case."

"Whatever you do is your business. I can't stop you from doing what you want to do, but I'm not talking about Justin. Sorry." It was obvious George didn't want to continue talking to Gary.

"I totally understand," Gary said for the second time as he crawled out of the office and returned to his car.

Gary didn't want to add any more emotional stress to George's life. He had his own way of dealing with the trauma of his son's murder and it hadn't changed much in over thirty years. His anger is still easily provoked; he is frozen at the same place he found himself when he didn't trust his emotions enough to attend Norman's parole hearings, or when, a few years earlier, a man he didn't know came into the shop and started asking him a series of pointed questions about Justin's murder. The man was persistent in his questioning and a bit obnoxious as George tried to convince him that he didn't discuss "anything with anybody about Justin."

"After awhile, my father got so upset that he actually went after the guy," Joey told Gary. "We had to physically pull him off the totally shocked jerk."

During an interview, Joey explained how difficult it is for George to thoroughly enjoy his grandchildren, especially Joey's five-year-old son, who is the spitting image of Justin.

"My dad will visit with us and look at my son and find it difficult to stay long because he sees Justin and it becomes painful for him."

George's suffering has obviously been constant. He has managed to survive by repressing all thoughts and avoiding all discussion of the horrid crime. Who is to say this is not the best way for George to deal with his pain?

After meeting with George, Gary was now at a crossroads. He decided to discontinue his research on the case and find something else to write about. Some friends wondered why he even wanted to undertake this project when it could be particularly upsetting to the victims.

He now understood why no one has researched the case or written a substantive story about it in over thirty years. He was resigned to back off and look for other creative pursuits in his golden years, instead of foolishly feeding his ego by trying to become a notable crime writer. The book's major purpose of sending a strong message to parents about today's need to be more vigilant in protecting their children unfortunately had to be sacrificed.

After several weeks had passed, Gary received a surprise message on his answering machine. It was from George. "Gary, I have been thinking about it and have decided I will buy one of those small tape recorders and make an audio tape for you. Give me a couple of months. I'll get back to you when I finish it."

Totally amazed, Gary quickly called George back and thanked him for his turnaround. George said that the memory of his courageous wife and the ordeal both of them went through should never be forgotten. He told Gary that the major reason he would provide an audiotape was to honor Jane's memory.

Almost four months passed and Gary never heard from George. He then called George and asked him how the tape was coming. George said he had tried to make the tape but found it a difficult and painful thing to do. Again, Gary told him he totally understood but asked him if he would be willing to answer a few questions in writing if Gary left the questions off in a sealed envelope at his office.

While George agreed, Gary felt the chances of George responding in writing were poor and probably as painful an exercise for George as the audiotaping was. However, one thing was now certain, Gary would continue his research and a book would be written honoring Jane Doherty with or without George's direct input.

Chapter 58

"A week doesn't go by when I don't think about this whole thing. It's a constant nightmare! If Norman Stedman gets released and comes around, I will kill him and plead insanity, and so would my father," a rage filled Joey Doherty told Gary.

Unlike his father, Joey was not reluctant to discuss the murder of his younger brother. In fact, Gary felt their discussions were somewhat therapeutic allowing Joey to vent some of his repressed anger and share his own perspectives on various aspects of the case; particularly how it has affected his own life and that of his family.

We were sitting in Joey's white service van in the parking lot of the Hopeville Fire Station, not far from his childhood home on Suffork Street where, as a seven-year-old, he had last played in the backyard with his younger brother Justin.

The three bay fire station was starting to show its age with small cracks and black mildew visible on the gray cinder blocks on each side of the building. Inside the bays sat three shiny red ladder trucks with their highly polished, shiny chrome contrasting with the bright fire red truck exteriors. Hopeville volunteer firemen like Joey and his father were part of a special, highly committed breed of men and a rich tradition that derived from many hours of camaraderie with fellow volunteer firemen over many decades. The station was a second home to volunteer fireman like Joey and his dad, and they felt comfortable there.

Joey was a hard working businessman in his late thirties with a new wife and a growing family of his own. He was a clean cut, solidly built, good-looking man with a cheerful personality, and as Gary quickly learned, strong opinions.

"My Mom and Dad were very strict with my sister and me after Justin's disappearance," he began.

"They wouldn't let us out of their sight. To this day, I am the same way, being overprotective of my young son and daughter. If my kids are outside playing, I'm in the yard with them. I don't want my son or daughter's name in the paper or for them to be given any special recognition at school. I try to keep our names out of the public spotlight. After what we have endured, we strongly protect our privacy."

Gary said, "You still appear to be very angry."

"Yes, I have had a real anger management problem for years and so has my dad."

"I am sorry to hear that, but I truly understand," Gary said.

Joey's voice softened. "I have talked with counselors, but it hasn't really helped. I still get worked up every time I think about what happened to my family and me. Why us, I keep asking myself? Justin was not the only victim of this terrible crime. My mom and dad, along with me, my sister, the Richmond family, and the Stedman family were all victims. It has deeply affected our lives. We're very close to the Richmonds and Donnie was my closest friend. We did everything together. We're so close that my mom and dad treated Donnie like another son."

"What else continues to haunt you?"

Joey's voice stared to quiver as it grew louder. "I learned to despise the press. They were horrible, hounding us and wanting every little detail! They wouldn't let us alone! When my mother died, we tried to have a private funeral. She had suffered so much throughout her life and now had lymphoma at age fifty. The cancer quickly spread to her brain and lungs and she died within a year of her diagnosis. It just wasn't fair.

"We planned a private graveside funeral with invited guests only. The funeral director did us a favor and put a small, innocuous obituary in the paper a day after the funeral. Did you hear me? A day after the funeral. When the press finally realized my mom was Justin Doherty's mother, they descended upon us like vultures. It was a day after the funeral and they wouldn't leave us alone as we grieved. And you wonder why I carry around all this repressed anger?"

As Gary got out of Joey's van and went back to his car, he had tremendous empathy for Joey and his family. A terrible memory consumes them and it won't go away. It is an agonizing memory that a number of families must live with each year, victims of a grisly crime that suddenly strikes them for no apparent reason. Lives change, relationships shatter and the pain endures. They do everything in their power to cope and continue on with their lives, but things are never the same.

Chapter 59

The auto body shop was an enlarged, two bay cinder block garage surrounded by abandoned cars on a lonely country road on the outskirts of Hopeville. When Gary entered the building, the strong smell of fresh paint flew up his nostrils. Several shiny new auto parts were randomly spread around the concrete floor, apparently waiting their turn to bring some old car back to life.

Gary was looking for the shop owner, Bud Richmond, when suddenly he appeared from underneath a badly dented 1992 Dodge van and warmly greeted him. At six-feet-four, he was a large, physically fit man with rosy cheeks, a full crop of light brown curly hair, and a welcoming smile. He reminded Gary of the muscular blacksmiths they used to cast in those cowboy movies years ago.

As Bud cleaned the grease off his hands, Gary noticed his son, Donnie, scurrying about in the other bay of the garage, eyeing him suspiciously. Gary shouted, "I would like to meet with you next, Donnie. Hopefully, we can go out to lunch and talk." Gary's intent was to talk to Bud and Donnie separately. Previously, he had talked with Donnie's mother, who agreed to encourage a reportedly reticent Donnie to meet with him. Meanwhile, Gary's objective was to have a "talking lunch" with Bud during his lunch break.

Bud hopped in Gary's car and drove about eight miles to a rustic looking restaurant where they found a quiet table on a far wall. The interior walls of the restaurant were knotty pine and the blond haired waitresses with their full, colorful blouses and flowing skirts made Gary feel like he was in some cozy chalet in the foothills of Vermont. The restaurant attracts tourists by the handful since it has the best food in town. Although hungry, Gary was also anxious to talk to Bud and get his take on the effect Norman's crime had on his family.

" You know Bud, Donnie appears to be bothered and not likely to talk to me."

"I don't know if he will talk with you or not. He has been terribly bothered with what happened to him with Stedman twenty-five years ago. It has affected his life in ways nobody will ever know. Donnie keeps a lot to himself. It surprises me that he doesn't view himself as a hero, the young man who helped expose the killer of Justin Doherty. That was what he was, you know, a hero."

"What do you mean?" Gary asked.

"It was not just a coincidence that Donnie was attacked by Stedman, triggering the eventual confession that followed when Stedman admitted killing Justin. I truly believe that God was working through Donnie and me to find an answer to what had happened to Justin. I also am totally convinced that he did work through us to identify the killer of that boy.

"It's funny, but I told Jane Doherty that when she finally learned what happened to Justin, she would be freed up from the heavy emotional burden she was carrying. She said I was the only one who said that to her. She didn't want to leave her home on Suffork Street but went along with George's wishes and moved down Center Street to his mom and dad's old house. Every time she passed Suffork she looked up the street and had a sad feeling and thought of the tree she had planted on the property memorializing her baby boy. She wondered if she might eventually go crazy never knowing what happened to him.

"Do you realize that when she and her family learned that Stedman had murdered Justin, she told me I was right? She said after the shock of knowing he was dead she experienced a warm and peaceful feeling. She could let go. She now knew Justin was in a better place."

Gary asked, "Was Jane a religious woman?"

"No, she wasn't in the formal sense, but she did find Christ before she died. I told the judge in the pre-trial hearing that it was divine intervention that caused us to expose Norman Stedman as the killer of Justin and finally give the family an answer to what happened to him. As horrible as the news was, the family could now find some peace."

"What did the judge say, Bud?"

"He didn't want to go there. In fact, he didn't want to hear a few things I said to him."

"Like what?"

"Well, the judge asked me what penalty I thought would be appropriate for Stedman given what he had done to Justin and tried to do to my son. I told him that he should definitely be given the death penalty. The judge indicated that might be a bit harsh since Massachusetts didn't even have the death penalty." I told him, 'You asked me what penalty I would give Stedman and I told you. If you didn't want to hear the answer, you shouldn't have asked me.'"

Bud's response to the judge made me smile. As the old timers say around town, "You can take the swamp Yankee out of Hopeville but you can't take the swamp out of the Yankee."

Later in the day, Gary interviewed Gloria Richmond at her home. She and Bud Richmond had sold the old family homestead on Suffork Street after divorcing several years before. As they sat at the kitchen table in her quaint white Cape Cod house, she was nervous and wanted to get the facts out as accurately as possible.

Gloria works full time as a school secretary. Both she and Bud have an amicable relationship and are still close to their children. They have similar ideas about how the incident with Norman Stedman has had a negative effect on Donnie's life. A youthful-looking and likeable woman with great verve, she explained it this way:

"Donnie never saw himself as a hero. In fact, he felt the other way and thought the Dohertys were upset with him. You have to realize that Donnie was extremely close to the Doherty family and still is. He and George are like father and son. Somehow, he felt extreme guilt and thought they would be mad at him. Don't ask me why, but that's how he felt. But do you know what those Dohertys did soon after they learned about their son's murder and how Stedman tried to strangle Donnie?"

"No, what?" Gary asked.

"They came to our house, all of them, and gave Donnie a gift and then hugged him. Can you imagine that? It was one of the most amazing gestures I have ever witnessed."

"Gloria, what memories do you have of Jane?"

"She was a wonderful woman, kind and lovable. The type of woman everyone liked. Unfortunately, I didn't see as much of her when the family moved to Center Street, but Bud, Donnie, George and Joey always remained close friends. I did visit Jane when she was in the hospital battling cancer. I couldn't believe how much that woman suffered in her lifetime."

It was obvious that Donnie Richmond has been haunted by the

fact that his life was nearly ended by Norman Stedman. He is now the divorced father of a young daughter and has had his personal struggles. Gary was anxious to talk to him and called him to schedule an interview. Unfortunately, he indicated he didn't want to talk and again Gary respectfully said that he understood.

Several weeks passed and Gary was sitting in the quiet of his den when his phone rang. It was Donnie. He sounded agitated and asked Gary why he was talking to his friends about him. Gary told him that he was not asking them any personal questions about him.

He explained that his only purpose was to get their impressions and descriptions of interactions they had with Norman as young boys. Gary mentioned that his mother thought he might want to talk to him and that's why he tried, although unsuccessfully, to interview him.

"My mother doesn't speak for me," he said. "Are you going to make big money writing this book? Is that why you are doing it?"

"No, that is not my motivation. I plan to explain my reasons in an author's note in the front of the book. I gave your parents and George and Joey Doherty a copy of my reasons for writing the book before I undertook this project. I also plan to give a draft of the manuscript to each family for their reaction before I send it to publishers.

I urge you to read it."

At this point, Donnie became extremely angry. "I will do everything, everything I can do to stop you from writing this book."

A young woman's voice then came on the line. "Donnie and I are meeting with a lawyer tomorrow to see what can be done to stop you from writing this book!"

Trying to maintain his composure Gary said, "Well, I'm sorry you feel that way. Go ahead and do what you have to do. I still plan on writing the book as truthfully and as sensitively as I can. Good night." With that, Gary hung up.

Chapter 60

Fred Stedman died in 1990 at the age of sixty-eight, just eight years after Norman's conviction and incarceration. He had married for the third time in 1985 and his new wife died within nine months. Still seeking companionship, he married his fourth wife two years later, a woman who was at least twenty-five years his junior.

He and his fourth wife, Nora, continued to live in the same house on Suffork Street until Fred passed away. His wife sold the house about two years after Fred's death, moved out of town and currently lives in a Boston suburb. After an exhaustive Internet search, Gary learned that Fred also had a sister who was still alive and lived out of state.

Gary called Fred's sister and her daughter answered the phone. He explained the reason for his call and told her he would like to talk with her mother the next day, if at all possible. They had a pleasant conversation and she confirmed the fact that Fred was her uncle and Norman was her first cousin. However, Gary noticed that she didn't respond when he asked if her mother had ever contacted Norman during his time in prison. Gary thought her silence might be due to her reluctance to speak for her mother on such a sensitive topic.

When he called the next day, he got the daughter again. The tone of her voice had changed considerably, now sounding somewhat unfriendly. She said her mother was really bothered by his call and didn't want to talk to him. She explained her family's need to protect their privacy and how terribly hurtful it is for them to discuss Fred and Norman's tragic lives. Gary received the impression that they wanted to erase the memory of Norman and not advertise the fact they were related to him. He told her he wouldn't bother her family again, but this time avoided saying, "I totally understand," because clearly he was disappointed in not being able to get vital information from Norman's closest living relatives.

His attempts to contact Nora, Fred's last wife, were also fruitless.

The telephone number provided by the Internet search and validated by the telephone long distance operator failed to connect. Her listed phone number was not in service and remained out of commission for a period of three months.

After making several unsuccessful calls, he finally gave up. It was unlikely she would have talked to him. Not living in Hopeville until marrying Fred in 1985, she had little to contribute except possibly some insights on how the crime affected Fred in the later stages of his life. For example, it would have been helpful if she could have shared how Fred felt after he visited his son in prison.

Throughout these ill-fated attempts, Gary felt very much like an intruder. While he completely understood why Norman's relatives didn't want to talk to him and honored their wishes, he was particularly disappointed that he couldn't get a more in-depth perspective on Norman's home life and his relationships with his father, grandmother, and step-mother.

Not all however was lost. In spite of his difficulty in getting important information from Fred's relatives, he was able to get feedback on Fred's later life from his pastor and other people in the community who knew him well.

After the sudden death of his third wife, Fred's life returned to some degree of normalcy when he married Nora. The two of them were active members of the Hopeville Baptist Church. Fred and his pastor paid periodic visits to Norman during the early years of his incarceration, traveling to prisons throughout New England and elsewhere, depending on where prison officials had moved Norman in order to shield his identity.

Fred could also be frequently seen at the local diner eating his meals and conversing in his polite and courteous manner with the "townies" he had known for years. Those acquaintances told Gary that Fred never mentioned his son in conversations with them.

One townie and fellow school janitor put it best, "Like his son, Fred had very few friends during his lifetime with the possible exception of his numerous wives. He was never a good communicator or shared any of his feelings. I know because we worked in the same school together for years and to be honest I felt like I hardly knew him. I did notice that after Norman's imprisonment his face always looked real sad and he rarely smiled. I wondered if he even talked to his new wife and shared his suffering with her. Although he never said so, I felt he grieved for his son. I could sense it. I really felt sorry for the poor guy. He was such a nice man in so many ways, but was dealt a bad hand in life."

Gary thought that Fred had to die with a heavy heart knowing what his son had done. He too was another sad victim in this crime. The premise that he knew about his son killing Justin at some point before the arrest was never proven, and it is unfair to suggest that Fred had purposely avoided turning him into the police. Unfortunately, that type of accusation is often directed at parents when one of their children commits a violent crime.

Gary also felt that it is equally unfair to suggest that Fred received preferential treatment from Hopeville police because of his past status as a reserve policeman. The facts indicate that with the exception of the Doherty house, the police didn't physically search the interior of any house on Suffork Street. They asked the owners to search their own houses, Fred's house included. Naturally, they believed Fred since he had high credibility as a former policeman, but they also believed all the closely-knit homeowners in the Suffork neighborhood who had followed the same procedure.

Depending on the nature of the search, it is also conceivable that even if the police had searched the Stedman house, they may have not discovered Justin's body since allegedly it was well hidden by Norman in his bedroom closet. Police were also not looking for a dead body at that time. Even if it had been in a trunk in the basement when volunteer fireman Todd Jenks conducted his search there the morning after Justin disappeared, Todd was not looking for a hidden body at that time either, but doing a visual inspection to see if Justin was somehow trapped in the cellar. As reported, he saw nothing, not even the trunks.

What is unknown about Fred Stedman is the role he played as a parent during the years when his son went from being a lonely boy to a child killer at the young age of sixteen.

Gary discovered that Fred's lack of cleanliness and his filthy house were manifestations of his life style and his son's. We know that the death of his first wife had a devastating effect on his nine-year-old son, Norman, who adored his mother. We also know that when he married his second wife and she and Fred's mother moved into his house, Norman had a contentious relationship with both women. Neighbors observed and reported these facts. They saw how Norman was treated and they heard the screaming and yelling when the two women tried to control him against his will.

As one of his classmates said, "Norman did not look like he was well kept." Or as one of his actor colleagues mentioned, "You wonder about Norman's childhood and the type of nurturing he got or didn't get at home."

In studies of people who become violent, children who are pathologically shy, have poor impulse control and whose quirks drive other kids away present a particular challenge to their parents.

As a college classmate observed, "Norman was like a pariah with other students who wanted nothing to do with him. Others were scared off by his strange looks and behavior." Such children by their late teens can become impulsive, hostile, socially anxious and friendless. They become particularly isolated and begin to blame others for their distress. The potential for violence heightens considerably. Such was the case with Norman Stedman.

Did Fred have the parental skills and knowledge to handle this type of challenge from his complicated and troubled son? Norman would have frustrated and baffled the best of parents. With proper parental and professional support though, could he have been saved from becoming a violent killer? We will never know.

What we do know is that Norman's aggression, resentment, and anger grew out of proportion and combined with his lack of impulse control resulted in him killing a helpless child. It is not unreasonable to think that the loss of his birth mother at his early age, the ensuing unhappiness and tension in his home life, and his constant rejection by both peers and adults played key roles in pushing him over the edge.

It is also apparent that Fred Stedman, his helpless father, had few answers. He was incapable of recognizing the violent tide that would engulf him. Gary wondered how Fred coped with the guilt and pain he must have felt seeing his son in one prison after another under protective custody. Hopefully, with the help of his Baptist faith and the support of his last wife, Fred somehow found a way to deal with his enormous grief.

Chapter 61

After all these years, Gary wondered if Norman Stedman is still singing his favorite song, *All By Myself,* when sitting in his prison cell.

He was all by himself during the first twenty-three-years of his life and is most likely still that way after decades behind prison walls. Is he still seething with rage and ready to explode? Is he still living inside his own bleak world? Is he indifferent to the feelings of others? Does he still seek notoriety? No one except prison authorities really knows.

Gary was still puzzled. Why were those people who knew Norman so blind? He fit the perfect criminal prototype. Only Clara Wright and Professor Trudy Light, two very perceptive women, realized how dangerous Norman was to others. Both of them warned other people and came close to notifying the authorities, but unfortunately did not in spite of their concerns.

Norman's dark writing revealed a sick young man crying for help but too proud and stubborn to seek it, as he rebuffed teachers and classmates who tried to help him, acting as if he enjoyed being a unique, bizarre personality. In one of his poems, he describes the futility he felt and sees his birthright as shameful and predestined to lead him to damnation.

In his short story where he creates an alien from another world who decides to remain on earth with his new love and their newborn son rather than return to his homeland, his fatalistic view of his life is in full view. Having grown in love with his adopted world, he eventually senses the first death throes and begins grieving. He gathers his Peggy and their son by his side as their lives tragically end with an explosion of light. How does anyone explain what led Norman to have such depressing thoughts, thoughts that parallel his early life where he is perceived as an alien in Hopeville and in college?

Gary also had another troubling question. What will happen to

Norman when he completes his prison sentence? It is unlikely that he will ever be granted parole before then, given the nature of his crime. Gary read that nearly eighty percent of respondents to a recent survey indicated a sexual offender should remain incarcerated until he is not a danger to society. But how is that to be determined?

Sexual offenders have a poor track record upon their release from prison. Significant improvement of a deep-rooted personality disorder like Norman's is rare and after forty years in prison his reintegration into society would be most difficult. Offenders imprisoned that long tend to revert to old mechanisms of coping like social withdrawal.

Gary agreed with Chief Velone that Norman would be better served remaining in a secure setting where he can receive the professional help and support he needs. Even if he meets the requirements established by the parole board, allowing Norman to walk the streets of Hopeville, or any community again, would have a real potential of putting innocent people in harm's way.

It is too bad that Norman's life and talents were wasted as they were. It is easy to blame his problem on a dysfunctional family situation, the loss of a loved one, low self-esteem brought on by rejection and personal ridicule, or some sort of biological anomaly. But many young men face these challenges in life without becoming killers.

In the final analysis, Norman's grotesque and unconscionable crime is a tragic case that has affected many and will continue to haunt the victims for the rest of their lives. As far as Jane and Justin Doherty and Fred Stedman are concerned, Gary hoped that they had finally found peace.

Chapter 62

It is unfortunate that Jane Doherty died before Gary had a chance to personally interview her. However, he talked at length with family members, friends and neighbors, and Rick Thurston, who knew her well. All parties agreed that she was a remarkable lady and a loving and caring mother. But they said she was also so much more—a beautiful woman who suffered greatly throughout her life, but in her suffering demonstrated a unique strength of character, courage, and faith.

Gary often wondered how he would have survived the loss of one of his children in a car accident or from a terminal illness or even if they had taken their own life. The death of a son or daughter at any age during the parents' lifetime is difficult, but the senseless murder of a young child is truly heartbreaking and must be the worst loss and searing pain a human being can ever endure.

Gary looked at the angelic and smiling face of his little five-year-old grandson in a picture on his desk wall and wondered how he would feel if he were kidnapped and murdered. How would he feel if he were missing for nearly seven years and then, when he was found, learned that his dead body had been grotesquely violated and all that remained was his shellacked skull and several bones? How would his mother and father feel? How would any member of the immediate family feel? Could they find the strength to put the pieces of their shattered lives back together again? Would their faith be strong enough to pull them through?

Although her mental torture was constant for twenty-five of her fifty years on earth, Jane Doherty was a ray of hope for those around her. She amazed the police with her graciousness, calm, and energy. Her pertinacity in trying to find her son was truly amazing. She talked openly to people about her missing son, keeping alive the hope that he would return to his family someday. She did everything in her power to assist the police in finding Justin and prior to the parole hearings led a one-woman crusade to keep his killer in jail. She was an inspiration to her family and to all the people of Hopeville. The only outward sign that she was still hurting occurred on her birthdays. She didn't celebrate them or allow the family even to mention them. It was on her birthday, May 18, 1975, that Justin was discovered missing when he didn't come home for dinner.

On a warm Indian summer day in late September 2000 about a dozen people in casual dress were holding hands around an open grave in Waterside Cemetery, a short walk down the street from the Doherty home on Center Street. Most of those in the funeral party wore dark shaded sunglasses to block the blazing sun that illuminated the headstones on the hundreds of graves in this hilly, serene historical cemetery. The rich smell of freshly cut green grass permeated throughout the beautiful resting place. A small group of family and close friends had just left a brief service at the funeral home and were now gathered to say their final good-byes to Jane Doherty, the woman everyone called, "Mom."

Jane had been diagnosed with lymphoma the previous February and her demise was swift. She had been rushed to the hospital on several occasions with excruciating pain during the past few months. She had suffered greatly.

Standing at the graveside for this private burial were George, Joey and his wife and family, Donnie Richmond and his family, Jane and George's sisters and brothers, and the Richmonds. Also in attendance was Jane's former daughter-in-law Diane. Robin Doherty was conspicuously absent. Nobody knew why she wasn't there, since she had attended the service at the funeral home. What is known is that she left Hopeville that day and never returned after making arrangements with Joey to care for her daughter. In the intervening years, the daughter has lived with Joey and his second wife and family.

Gary asked Diane if she could recall what thoughts were going through her mind as they stood at the grave.

"I guess we kept asking ourselves, 'Why, Why?' How much tragedy and pain can one family endure in a lifetime? We specifically asked how this could happen to such a caring and compassionate mother who loved and closely protected her children with her whole being. We realized that what happened to the Dohertys was out of their control, but we still asked, 'Why?' We were looking for answers, but there were none."

Diane shared her personal feelings about the woman she clearly admired greatly.

"She was an awesome woman and a friend to all. She loved children and embraced all types of people regardless of their race or socio-economic status. I was her former daughter-in-law, but even after the divorce from Joey she was my best friend; she was the best of the best. I called her 'Mom' something my own mother understood and readily accepted. The fact that the Doherty family can come through all this tragedy and grief in one piece shows that all of them are strong people and real survivors. They are amazing; however, the strongest and the most amazing was Jane. She led the way and the rest of the family got their strength from her."

"Losing Jane must have been a great loss to the family," Gary said.

"Yes, it was. But do you know something? It is now Justin's turn to have Jane. Yes, to finally have his mother. I think all of us around that grave realized that and it gave us peace."

Chapter 63

It was early morning and Gary was sitting in his car outside the old Stedman homestead. Raindrops splattered on his car windows as water streamed hurriedly down the narrow street. Gary looked intently at the weather beaten mill houses once occupied by the Stedman and Doherty families. He spotted the roadside curb in front of the Stedman house where Norman had sat for hours smoking a cigarillo and intently watching the young neighborhood children playing across the street in Tracey's Field. Gary was in a reflective mood trying to understand how such a horrible crime could occur in this peaceful, close-knit neighborhood. Why did God let something like this happen?

He had finally completed his research on the kidnapping and murder of young Justin Doherty and written the first draft of his book. But he still felt ambivalence about publishing the manuscript.

He was punishing himself by thinking, "Am I causing more harm than good? If what I have written is upsetting to the victims, should I just tear it up and forget the whole project?" He decided he needed to share his manuscript with the victims and get their reactions before proceeding any further. As promised beforehand, he definitely wouldn't use real names in the book and would protect the victims' privacy as much as he could.

Yet, he was still bothered. He had unveiled some information not previously known about the crime, but may have raised more questions than he answered. Still, he hoped his central message to parents and other readers would be understood, heeded, and appreciated in this day of increased violence and increased concern for the safety of our precious children and grandchildren.

Undoubtedly, he had shed some light on a number of questions about Norman's anti-social personality and what might have motivated him to brutally kill a young boy and desecrate his dead body. He was able to discover some unknown facts about the role of the Hopeville police in the case and clarify some of the mistakes they made in their investigation. And finally, he was able to examine how this awful crime affected its victims.

But there still remained unanswered questions, mostly about Fred Stedman and Norman's relationship with his father, stepmother, and grandmother. The refusal of Donnie Richmond and Fred's sister to talk to him, although understandable in some respects, also raised some new questions in his mind. The failure to locate Robin Doherty and Nora Stedman and get their first-hand perspectives, as well as being rebuffed by the State Department of Corrections in his request to contact Norman, unquestionably limited his research and insight into the crime.

Of course, the major missing piece in better understanding this crime is Norman's sealed journal. What exactly did Norman say in that infamous bluebook that has so shocked those few people who have read it? The rumors that persist are still just rumors in spite of some guarded responses given by Chief Velone and Detectives Thurston and Harrison to questions that he posed; however, their responses did allow him to make some reasonable assumptions about the journal's contents.

But isn't this what life is about? You are never able to get all the facts and details and get to the full truth, particularly on sensitive personal matters. People fight for their privacy and as a result certain key information is never revealed to the public. This is their right and Gary had respected that right.

However, there is one unanswered question that especially haunts Gary. The mourners who stood at Jane Doherty's open grave at the Waterside Cemetery asked it. Why does a conscientious, loving mother who protected her shy, highly dependent child at every turn have to suffer the way Jane Doherty did?

Clara Wright, the Hopeville librarian and Community Theatre Player colleague of Norman's who knew him as well as anyone could have had the answer. She approached Gary in the supermarket one day after he had finished his research on the case. He briefly shared his findings with her since she had been so gracious in her interview weeks before. During the conversation, he mentioned how unfair it was that Jane Doherty and her family had to suffer the way they did.

Clara mentioned a passage from John Gardner's, *Nickel Mountain*, which speaks to the awesome responsibility a parent has in raising a child. She thought the quotation might provide helpful insight to the question Gary kept asking himself. She could not remember the exact quote but promised him she would set the book aside and he could pick it up later that afternoon.

Gary walked up the steps of the old stone library, a magnificent building given to the town by a local philanthropist two hundred years ago. As he entered the room where the front desk was located, the special musty smell that old libraries have overcame him. He looked around at the handsome oak walls and his eyes focused on the stage where the productions of the Community Players were held many years before. He visualized a beefy Norman springing up from that pile of putrefied leaves.

Clara got his attention and gave him the book to check out. He quickly found a comfortable library chair and opened the page she had marked.

One of the main characters in the book, Henry Soames, is remembering what his friend George Loomis said to him the time his son Jimmy had suffered convulsions. George spoke of the awesome responsibility a parent has and how you would do anything to protect the child you love. After he says that, George remembers something. He realizes that you really can't totally protect your child and you're only recourse is to turn to God.

As he left the library, Gary's eyes met Clara's. He shook his head and blew her a kiss and left.

It occurred to Gary that the passage Clara gave him clearly captured the major reason he decided to write his book. He wanted people to know the story of how one courageous woman lived with special grace and dignity through an ordeal few people in a lifetime experience. And more importantly, he wanted them to know how an evil crime led that remarkable woman to God and eternal life with her son, Justin. Her memory should never be forgotten.

Postscript

Nearly two years after the completion of this book, the press reported that the killer, alias Norman Stedman, was scheduled for release from prison in August, 2011. According to the Department of Corrections, Norman had accumulated twelve years of "good time" and would be given his freedom after having served only twenty-eight years of his forty year sentence. The news sent angry shock waves throughout Hopeville and the state. How can society let a deranged killer of a small child who did gruesome things to the dead child's body go back on the streets again? A killer who at age twenty-three tried to kill another young boy? The victims and general public wanted answers.

Clearly mental illness research done on murderers still can't provide us with definitive reasons on why a sociopath like Norman turns violent. Yes, we look for biological and psychological deviations and certain set behaviors.

We look for clues to those human experiences that contribute to twisted anti-social personalities—experiences such as child abuse, lack of parental love and proper nurturing, and cruel and constant rejection that permanently damages a young person's self image, self worth, and sexual identity while at the same time repressing their anger and guilt. These are unfortunate ingredients that can later develop into an outbreak of uncontrollable rage and violence. Gary found that some of these patterns were apparent in Norman's youth, but no one can fully explain why one sociopath kills a small child while others with the same background don't.

Gary learned that rehabilitating criminals like Norman is quite perplexing. Noted mental health professionals appear to be engaged in guesswork. Is there any assurance that a killer like Norman after completing twenty-eight years in prison will not kill again? What constitutes rehabilitation of a cagey, calculating, intelligent criminal like Norman? Making decisions to release inmates who have committed capital crimes is a risky business like playing Russian roulette.

Rehabilitation is a laudable goal. However, we also have to admit that in some cases rehabilitation is not possible because the mental damage is so deep that it is irreversible and beyond repair. This surely appears to be the case with Norman Stedman.

We are still at the point of needing improved research and increased focus on rehabilitation to better inform parole board members and medical personnel before they make professional judgments and release criminals of violent capital crimes and send them back into the public arena. Why take such a risk with a killer who committed one of the most heinous, bizarre, and unspeakable crimes imaginable?

Norman should have been sentenced to life without parole and clearly would receive that sentence today. Although well meaning, the plea bargain has proven to bring more continuing and intense pain to the Dohertys with the tortuous parole situations and now the announcement of Norman's intended release from prison.

The public release of the bluebook (the sealed journal) contents and a life sentence for Norman without parole in 1982 could have resulted in some finality to this crime. At this point, it may be the right time to unseal the infamous bluebook if it will result in keeping Norman institutionalized.

Some people will say, "The law is the law." The man has paid for his crime, completed his sentence, and has a legal right to walk out of the prison a free man subject only to ten years of parole. He doesn't even have to register as a sexual offender. That is the law.

But is Norman a danger to himself and to others? What real evidence and assurance exists that he has been rehabilitated? The victims have a right to know. It just doesn't make sense putting this type of killer back on the streets. His release may be putting the general public at great risk especially young children.

The state civil statues on mental health need to be followed and a comprehensive evaluation of Norman by highly competent psychiatrists must be conducted to determine if he is suffering from mental illness. This is another reason for the court to publicly release the sealed journal or at least allow the psychiatrists to read it. Remember, according to handwriting experts, Norman was an adult when he wrote the journal from his old notes.

If the psychiatric evaluation finds Norman mentally ill and

determine that he it would be dangerous to release him, he would continue to be institutionalized and receive professional help.

Unfortunately, the possible release of Norman Stedman will add to the persisting pain, anger, and suffering still present in the minds and hearts of the living victims of this crime. Jane Doherty is at peace and her spirit, determination, and courage will live on. Fred Stedman's life ended in great sorrow as he witnessed his son arrested, condemned, and sent to prison as a child killer and prayed for his salvation.

George Doherty, however, is now at a different point of anguish. He is so angered and distraught that he has publicly spoken for the first time about his son's kidnapping and murder since the search in 1975. He is now seeking revenge. In a surprising change in character, George is demanding that the contents of the sealed bluebook be made public and is threatening to kill Norman and "inflict the type of pain to the killer like he did to my son." He feels he has a right to the document and plans to seek legal assistance to get the court to unseal it as part of a crusade to keep Norman in prison.

Although currently shaken by the possible release of Norman in what appears to be a huge mistake, we pray that the remaining members of the Doherty and Richmond families will eventually find peace in the years ahead and be able to live normal lives free from haunting memories such tragedies create. They have suffered enough.

Acknowledgements

I am deeply indebted to Judy Robinson, Dan Groves, and Michael Pesta for their helpful assistance during the writing and editing of this book and a former editor and close friends who convinced me that my book was an important and compelling story that needed to be read, especially by parents of young children.

Special thanks also go to Gerry Goldstein for his review and reaction to my developing manuscript. Gerry was the reporter who covered the crime for twenty-five years for the *Narragansett Times* and *Providence Journal* and provided me with newspaper articles relating to the actual crime and its aftermath. In the book, all articles are mentioned as appearing in the *Hopeville Times*. I thank him for allowing me the use of his material and his amazing recall of important details and events that occurred during the course of the crime.

Credit is also given to Norman's former theatre classmate and *Pawtucket Times* reporter for his article regarding Norman's poetry.

Finally, I would like to thank the real members of the Doherty and Richmond families, their Suffork Street neighbors, the Chief of Police and those members of the Hopeville police department, especially the real Rick Thurston and his detectives, who provided critical details about the actual crime. Special thanks go to the good people of Hopeville who graciously agreed to be interviewed and provided me with valuable information about a sad and brutal crime most of them wanted to forget.

About the Author

Dr. William R. Holland is a veteran public educator, Professor Emeritus at Rhode Island College in Providence, Rhode Island, and was a school superintendent for twenty years in both Massachusetts and Rhode Island. Later in his career, he served as Executive Director of the Rhode Island Principals Association and Rhode Island Commissioner of Higher Education.

He is the author of three previous books, *Selecting School Leaders (2006)*, *The Making of a School Superintendent (2007)*, *A School in Trouble: A Personal Story of Central Falls High School (2010)*.

Now retired, he and his family live in southern Rhode Island where he remains active as an author and consultant.

CPSIA information can be obtained at www.ICGtesting.com
262250BV00004B/8/P